T0129625

Living ABOVE THE SNAKE LINE

A Unique Perspective on the
Present-Day Deliverance Ministry of Jesus Christ

James Maloney

WESTBOW
PRESS®
A DIVISION OF THOMAS NELSON
& ZONDERVAN

Disclaimer: The author is not a medical professional and recognizes that there are people who need to seek medical and psychiatric help, apart from spiritual issues. The contents of this book are not to be construed as medical or psychiatric advice, nor are they intended to diagnose any health issues or provide treatment for such. If you are under the care of a mental or physical health care professional, do not stop taking medication until you have cleared it with your doctor.

Greek/Hebrew citations from Strong, J. (1890). Strong's exhaustive concordance of the Bible. Abingdon Press.

Scripture taken from the New King James Version. Copyright © 1979, 1980, 1982 by Thomas Nelson, Inc. Used by permission. All rights reserved.

Scripture taken from the King James Version of the Bible.

Scripture taken from the Amplified Bible, copyright © 1954, 1958, 1962, 1964, 1965, 1987 by The Lockman Foundation. Used by permission.

WestBow Press books may be ordered through booksellers or by contacting:

WestBow Press
A Division of Thomas Nelson & Zondervan
1663 Liberty Drive
Bloomington, IN 47403
www.westbowpress.com
1 (866) 928-1240

Because of the dynamic nature of the Internet, any web addresses or links contained in this book may have changed since publication and may no longer be valid. The views expressed in this work are solely those of the author and do not necessarily reflect the views of the publisher, and the publisher hereby disclaims any responsibility for them.

Any people depicted in stock imagery provided by Thinkstock are models, and such images are being used for illustrative purposes only. Certain stock imagery © Thinkstock.

ISBN: 978-1-5127-2020-4 (sc)
ISBN: 978-1-5127-2021-1 (e)
Library of Congress Control Number: 2015918880

Print information available on the last page.

WestBow Press rev. date: 12/9/2015

To the late David Alsobrook, a mentor and a true friend.

Contents

"How you are fallen from heaven,
O Lucifer, son of the morning!
How you are cut down to the ground,
You who weakened the nations!
For you have said in your heart:
'I will ascend into heaven,
I will exalt my throne above the stars of God;
I will also sit on the mount of the congregation
On the farthest sides of the north;
I will ascend above the heights of the clouds,
I will be like the Most High.'
Yet you shall be brought down to Sheol,
To the lowest depths of the Pit.
Those who see you will gaze at you,
And consider you, saying:
'Is this the man who made the earth tremble,
Who shook kingdoms,
Who made the world as a wilderness
And destroyed its cities,
Who did not open the house of his prisoners?'"

—Isaiah 14:12-17

1

Satan Has Been Defeated Your Whole Life

atan is a defeated foe. If you've been a follower of Christ for any length of time at all, you know this, at least on some level. You understand the biblical concept that the works of the enemy of your soul were brought to no effect upon Christ's death on the cross. What the devil had intended to be his greatest victory—the death of God Himself— was turned back upon him, and he found himself crushed under the heel of God's Son, to whom all authority in heaven, and on earth, and below the earth, and on the sea, was given. (Matthew 28:18; Revelation 5:13) When Jesus died, Satan's power was stripped. When the Lord was raised from the dead and exalted by the Father, it solidified Jesus' place for all eternity over Lucifer, the fallen son of the morning.

"Therefore God also has highly exalted Him and given Him the name which is above every name, that at the name of Jesus every knee should bow, of those in heaven, and of those on earth, and of those under the earth, and that every tongue should confess that Jesus Christ is Lord, to the glory of God the Father." (Philippians 2:9-11)

One of the greatest "keys of the kingdom of heaven" is the revelation that God the Father gave Peter in Matthew 16:13-20;

that is, Jesus Christ is the Son of the living God. It's upon this rock that Jesus said His church would be built, and the gates of Hades would not prevail against it. The believer's authority to "bind and loose" is rooted firmly in the understanding that Christ has defeated every entity of hell, including the prince of lies, Satan. Our Lord is a conquering King, a total Victor, and the fact is that Satan has been defeated for your entire life! He is an utterly vanquished and subjugated tyrant. He is *not* the same devil that he used to be!

There are many books on deliverance out there, and the vast majority of them have great merit. But what will make this book unique (and prayerfully important) is we approach the concept of deliverance from the standpoint that we are facing a muzzled, broken foe. I cannot state this clearly enough—demons are *already* defeated. They have no authority or power in our lives, as believers in Jesus, save what we choose to give them. It's not like some days the devil is winning, and sometimes God is winning—a back and forth struggle, and poor humanity is stuck in the middle of clashing tides of angelic and demonic hosts. That is an errant philosophy.

Yes, I am aware that Satan is the prince of the power of the air (Ephesians 2:2), and that this world system is corrupted by his activity. That word "prince" in the Greek means the one who is in the first position of rank—the chief ruler or commander. (See Strong's #758.) "Power" here is authority or jurisdiction. (See Strong's #1849.) The word "air"—which, appropriately enough, is the word *aer* ("ah-air," Strong's #109)—means the lower, denser atmosphere closest to the earth. It is the air that we breathe, not the upper, rarified air as we approach space.

In other words, Satan is the chief ruler over the jurisdiction of this earthly realm. He doesn't *own* it; he is merely operating in delegated (or rather, pilfered) authority that was given to him by Adam when the man sinned.

I know that there are skirmishes in the unseen atmosphere between angels and demons, as the fallen foe tries to reassert dominion over their regional areas of influence, and that we do "wrestle... against spiritual hosts of wickedness in the heavenly places." (See Daniel 10:10-14 and Ephesians 6:10-13) But concerning you and me, who are born-again, blood-purchased followers of Jesus Christ—not "children of disobedience"—our adversary has no rights over us, excepting what we choose to yield to him by rebellion against our Lord.

Can the enemy try to harass you? Yes. Does this mean your life is all roses and cupcakes? No. Can the enemy test your defenses, look for broken hedges, generally be a nuisance? Can the enemy try your faith? Of course. Otherwise there would be no need to write a book such as this, and there would be no reason to include the Book of Job in the canon of scriptures. But this does not negate the truth that Christ made a mockery of Satan's principality and power at the cross (Colossians 2:15), nor does it change the hard fact that, "...the God of peace will crush Satan under your feet shortly. The grace of our Lord Jesus Christ be with you. Amen." (Romans 16:20)

Peace is used as a crushing weapon—isn't that a strange visual?

Grace is used as a bludgeon to smash our enemy to the ground and place him under our feet. It is from this standpoint that we address the theology of deliverance.

Your victory is assured. Our Lord has established an overcoming kingdom that already abides within you as a follower of Him. Genesis 26:15-18 shows Isaac re-digging his father's wells after Abimelech acknowledges the son of Abraham is mightier than he. I believe this applies to us as well—that we have a mandate from God to enforce the demonstration of our authority over the enemy. Isaac was showing his dominion over the Philistines by undoing the works they had done. It is the same for us. We have been given the authority to exercise dominance and lordship over our enemy, and we show this by re-digging the wells of salvation (which include healing, deliverance, etc.) they had stopped up by sin, sickness, division, and death.

Isaiah 14 tells us that we will "narrowly look" upon our foe and consider: "Is *this* what we've been afraid of?" I paraphrase, but I believe that is the intent of the passage in its context: you have no reason to be fearful of any demon in hell, for the Lord has put them all under your feet!

The Destruction of Satan

First John 3:8 says, "He who sins is of the devil, for the devil has sinned from the beginning. For this purpose the Son of God was manifested, that He might destroy the works of the devil." Jesus came to earth—yes, to save us, but moreover to demolish the works of the enemy. To disarm, to defeat, to *crush* the works of the devil. The Greek verb for "might destroy" is *lyo* ("loo-oh," Strong's #3089), and it is defined "to loosen," as in to untie shoelaces. But it also means much more: "to dissolve" (as in breaking up a marriage); "to set free" (as a prisoner is released); "to undo bandages" (things that constrict the movement of the body); "to dismiss or break up an assembly; to unmake laws; to annul, subvert, to do away with; to deprive of authority; to declare unlawful; to loose what is compacted or built together, to break up, demolish; to dissolve something coherent into parts, to destroy; to overthrow."

It is of interesting note that this is the same word as "loose" in Matthew 16:19. We have been given these keys for overcoming the works of the enemy.

And for further contemplation, consider that Jesus Christ was manifested to *divorce* us from a "marriage" with Satan. If "he who sins is of the devil, for the devil has sinned from the beginning," it stands to logical reason those in the world are "wedded," after a fashion, to the father of sins; but when we are brought into the Lord's kingdom as His Bride, that connection with our old husband is annulled and dissolved, for Christ has *lyo*'d the works of the devil.

One last thought concerning this powerful Greek word:

"But the day of the Lord will come as a thief in the night, in which the heavens will pass away with a great noise, and the elements will melt with fervent heat; both the earth and the works that are in it will be burned up. Therefore, since all these

5

things will be dissolved, what manner of persons ought you to be in holy conduct and godliness, looking for and hastening the coming of the day of God, because of which the heavens will be dissolved, being on fire, and the elements will melt with fervent heat?" (2 Peter 3:10-12)

Lyo is used in this passage for the first instance of "melt" (Verse 10) as well as both instances of "dissolved." The second instance of "melt" in Verse 12 is the word for "to make liquid, to perish or become destroyed by melting." (See Strong's #5080.) But the point I wish to make is that "the earth and the works that are in it will be burned up." These worldly works are melted with a fervent heat in the day of the Lord.

The Lord was manifested to devastate the works of the devil entirely, so that we might be able to reflect the image of Christ totally in Him. The destruction was unmitigated when Christ died. (I'll talk about His resurrection in a bit.) The influence of Satan against a child of God is loosened, undone, dissolved! I am convinced that Satan is working in a self-delusional state of victory, and this is the approach I take every time I am confronted with a deliverance need.

I know 1 Peter 5:8 says, "Be sober, be vigilant; because your adversary the devil walks about like a roaring lion, seeking whom he may devour." He still prowls around, looking for easy prey, and he *can* enslave those who yield to him. But he has *no power* over the redeemed, so long as we don't give him an advantage over us, so long as we don't come into agreement with him. This is why Peter admonishes us to be sober and vigilant, not running scared from the big, bad lion, but enforcing the victory that Jesus won on our behalf by being mindful of not walking right into the lion's open mouth.

"...Nor give place to the devil." (Ephesians 4:27) This means do not give him a place of occupancy or any position of influence—do not give him the *opportunity* to devour you!

Now, Jesus not only came to destroy the devil's works, He came to destroy the devil himself.

"Inasmuch then as the children have partaken of flesh and blood, He Himself likewise shared in the same, that through death He might destroy him who had the power of death, that is, the devil, and release those who through fear of death were all their lifetime subject to bondage." (Hebrews 2:14-15)

Notice it is those who "through fear of death" were all their lifetime subjected to bondage. The point in this passage is that Christ came to *destroy* as well as *release*.

"...But has now been revealed by the appearing of our Savior Jesus Christ, who has abolished death and brought life and immortality to light through the gospel..." (2 Timothy 1:10)

This verse says Christ abolished death. We see that Christ destroyed him who had the power of death. Who did He come to destroy? The devil. In destroying one (the devil) you have to destroy the other (death.) Now before you get some wonky notion I'm saying that we all can live forever on this earth and never physically die, I want to point out that "abolished" is the Greek word *katargeo* ("kah-tar-gay-oh," Strong's #2673). It is a compound word formed from *kata* (Strong's #2596, a preposition meaning "according to" or "toward") and *argeo* (Strong's #691, "idle, barren, inactive, delayed" from a root meaning "lazy, lingering, unemployed"). This word is sometimes translated "cumber," "do away," "cease," or "destroy" in the New Testament, but it is not speaking of *annihilation*. Let's be honest, both the devil and death still do exist in our world, right? But *katargeo* speaks of "taking out of operational existence."

It means to *paralyze*—"to render idle, unemployed, inactive, inoperative; to cause a person or thing to have no further efficiency; to deprive of force, influence, power; to cause to cease, put an end to, do away with, annul, abolish; to cease, to pass away, be done away; to be severed from, separated from, discharged from, loosed from any one; to terminate all intercourse with one."

So we are speaking of spiritual death here—the consequences of sin; that is, infirmity, sickness, poverty, disease. Death has been rendered inoperative by Christ; the devil has been put into a permanent "idle" state to those who *abide* in Christ! (We'll discuss some keys to abiding in Christ a little later.)

But for now, let me give you an example. First Peter 2:24 says, "...by whose stripes you were healed." Past tense. Were healed. Meaning, this is a done deal, already finished, it *has* happened. But how many know you can still be sick and have the symptoms of an infirmity? Why? Because sickness and death aren't annihilated (yet), but as you appropriate the victory of Christ on the cross, you render their effects inoperative, inactive, paralyzed.

So we have a job to do. That is to make the devil *unemployed*. Spiritual death and its consequences are to have no effect on us.

"And this I say, that the law, which was four hundred and thirty years later, cannot annul the covenant that was confirmed before by God in Christ, that it should make the promise of no effect... You have become estranged from Christ, you who attempt to be justified by law; you have fallen from grace." (Galatians 3:17; 5:4)

A Public Spectacle

Go back to Colossians 2:15. "Having disarmed principalities and powers, He made a public spectacle of them, triumphing over them in it."

Follow with me here for just a bit. In Genesis 3, God pronounces a curse upon man. "In the sweat of your face you shall eat bread, till you return to the ground, for out of it you were taken; for dust you are, and to dust you shall return." (Verse 19) We are dust. Dead skin cells flake off, float in the air—that's dust. Yuck.

In Verse 14, God curses the serpent (that is, the devil): "... Because you have done this, you are cursed more than all cattle, and more than every beast of the field; on your belly you shall go, and you shall eat dust all the days of your life."

What does the devil eat? Dust. That's us. Our dead flesh because of the curse of sin.

But read Verse 15: "And I will put enmity between you and the woman, and between your seed and her Seed; He shall bruise your head, and you shall bruise His heel."

9

"Seed" in the New King James is capitalized, because it's referring to Christ Himself.

Now you probably know in Roman times, when Caesar defeated a foe (rather, when his generals did)—the vanquished was paraded before the people, usually stripped and tied to the back end of a donkey. This was a "triumph." The root of this word is pagan: singing a noisy song to Bacchus/Dionysus—the god of wine and merriment. It's also where we get "trump card" and "trumpet." The Romans made a loud, noisy processional of a defeated foe—a public spectacle of the conquered enemy.

Jesus made a triumph of Satan when He died on the cross. When Satan "bruised His heel," (the body of His flesh) Christ crushed his head. And a serpent whose head's been crushed cannot strike or eat—his means of consuming dust (our flesh) has been paralyzed. That is the theme for this book: we can live above the Snake Line (we'll explain that as the book goes on.)

We need to have a new understanding and perspective about the cross. God the Father viewed Christ as the Victor *in death*! He saw the cross as the place where Satan lost, not Jesus. "In it" (the cross) is where Jesus triumphed over the principalities and powers of our enemy. Notice, it's not in His resurrection, but His death!

Christ's resurrection demonstrated that His victory was all-inclusive and comprehensive. Paul says Jesus was, "...declared to be the Son of God with power, according to the Spirit of holiness, by the resurrection from the dead..." (Romans 1:4) That "with power" is how Jesus was able to strike the enemy's head and break the serpent's fangs.

But here is where it's so awesome for you and me: then, after He was raised from the dead, He turned around and handed His victory *to us*! "...We are more than conquerors through Him who loved us." (Romans 8:37) "More than conquerors." Here's another Greek compound word: *hypernikao* ("hoo-per-nee-kah-oh, Strong's #5245). You probably recognize *hyper*, as in hyperactive, hyperbole, hypercaffeinated, or hyperdrive for you Trekkies. It's a preposition that means "over, above, beyond, exceedingly, abundantly, very highly, more than." (Strong's #5228)

You might or might not know that the second word, *nikao*, comes from the root *nike*. (Strong's #3529) Yes, like the tennis shoe, but the Greeks pronounced it "nee-kay." The Greek letters are νίκη, and it's where we get the word "victory." It was the name of the goddess of victory—in Rome she was called Victoria, appropriately enough. It's also where we get the names Nicholas and Veronica. At the Grecian Olympics, the winner of an event was given an olive branch and declared "*hypernikao*"—a super athlete—one who was more than a conqueror, the very best of all competitors.

That's us. We didn't have to fight this war (the overall battle)—we just fight smaller skirmishes to enforce the triumph Christ already won. We need to have an understanding that we go into battle as *victors beforehand*. We are already hyper-nikes.

Think of two main armies clashing on the wide open plains of a battlefield. Even if one side utterly decimates the other, and the overall conquest is assured and total, there may still be individuals skirmishing on the outlands of the battle zone amongst the trees.

We're those people, fighting on the fringes against an enemy that doesn't know it's already lost—or has deluded itself into thinking there's still a chance they might win. We're on "mop up" duty, so to speak.

You know, there *are* people experiencing victory in Christ. We *are* supposed to have a steadfast overcoming walk in the Lord. We *are* supposed to receive answers to prayers and live in a state of inner peace from day-to-day. That is not to browbeat anyone—all of us suffer momentary setbacks in this life, the occasional defeat, because we are not yet perfected in Christ. But that is to be the rare exception, not the norm. It is not to undo the general state of all-around victory that He wants us to live in. So that's why books of this nature are important: to help you, in some way, recognize your place as more than an conqueror. The Lord has handed His olive branch to you, and you are supposed to walk it out as one who has overcome all your adversaries. Jesus has given you the keys to the kingdom to press your rights as a victor over a defeated foe.

There cannot be any other outcome. You have no choice but to win. "Now thanks be to God who always leads us in triumph in Christ..." (2 Corinthians 2:14) Always. Not sometimes. In light of the section earlier about what "leading a triumph" means, you have to know that "in Christ" there is a celebration victory for you, even though you didn't fight the battle yourself. It's like we're the Caesars of old, and Jesus is our great General. He went out and fought for us, then paraded the defeated enemy before our feet. We didn't have to fight the battle—our Lord gained the victory for us!

Look, dear reader, don't wait until Satan is standing before God's tribunal before you believe he is defeated. I am convinced that those who will "look narrowly" upon him in that day will be a little miffed at themselves for having feared him and lived a defeated life—all as a result of *believing a lie.* I think they'll feel a little cheated and embarrassed, tricked by a hissing snake whose head has been crushed. Don't be one of those people. I weary of listening to people magnify the devil and puff him up into something he is not—what fools he is making of them!

"Do you not know that we shall judge angels?" (1 Corinthians 6:3) There is great reward in heaven for those who receive this truth in life, who are not intimidated by a spirit of unbelief that says, "If I engage, I'll be set up for disappointment, destruction, devastation." Stop believing a lie. The devil is not the problem. We must look elsewhere. The enemy you are "battling" has already been defeated—permanently—by One who is much greater than you!

*"He who dwells in the secret place of the Most High
Shall abide under the shadow of the Almighty.
I will say of the Lord, 'He is my refuge and my fortress;
My God, in Him I will trust.'"*

—*Psalm 91:1-2*

2

Hidden

The 91st Psalm will be a keynote passage for this book. It is one of the most well-known, beloved psalms, of which many of us have whole passages—if not its entirety—memorized. It is quoted ever and anon, one of the most uplifting and comforting passages in all of scripture. Spurgeon recounted, "A German physician was wont to speak of it as the best preservative in times of cholera, and in truth, it is a heavenly medicine against plague and pest. He who can live in its spirit will be fearless, even if once again London should become a lazar-house, and the grave be gorged with carcases." (See *The Treasury of David*, C.H. Spurgeon.)

The author of the psalm is not exactly known—it may have been David; it may have been Moses. Probably the latter. In any case, the intent and message of this endearing psalm, while simple in its poetic beauty, is underpinned by some of the deepest truths about God's nature and how we are to interact with that nature. We know that the Bible is the message God has given to the world on how mankind may discern Him, and Psalm 91 is one of the most enlightening teachings in the entirety of the Word. So, I think it will be fitting in a book about Jesus' present-day deliverance ministry, and how we can live a life of victory above the Snake Line, to take some time and study Psalm 91 out.

Elevation

Before we begin, let me define what I mean by "living above the Snake Line." This phrase is not unique to me. The first person I heard it from was my late brother-in-law, David Alsobrook—just before his passing, I asked his permission to use the phrase as the title for the book, and obviously he agreed. When I started looking up "snake lines," apart from the plumber's tool, I realized there have been other theological teachings presented using a similar concept, so I don't think it will be possible to find out where it originated from. However, from a natural standpoint, there is a general notion founded on ancient tradition that at a certain altitude above sea level, poisonous snakes do not reside. With very few exceptions, this holds true.

There is certainly anecdotal evidence of such from yours truly. I grew up in a resort community named Idyllwild, California, in the San Jacinto Mountains above Palm Springs. San Jacinto Peak, the highest point in the range, is just under 11,000 feet. That's pretty high up there. Now, tree lines vary geographically, but for most of the United States, it's around 10,000 feet above sea level, give or take. After that, either the cold or the lack of moisture prohibits the majority of trees from growing, hence "tree line." It is at this level the so-called snake line exists.

My hometown is at 5,400 feet, appropriately called "Mile

High Idyllwild." In my youth, I saw rattlesnakes there and had a couple treacherous run-ins with the nasty critters during my hikes and climbs. However, I never encountered a snake at the tree line, nor have I ever met anyone who lives there who did. To the best of my knowledge, there are no poisonous snakes at the top of the mountain.

How does this tie in spiritually? I'm glad you asked. I believe there is a place that we can get to in our walk with the Lord that the poisonous vipers and the roaring lions—the devil and his demonic cronies—cannot reach you. It is a place where you are so "hidden in Christ"(Colossians 3:3) that you are actually preserved from the wily tricks of the devil. The fowler's snare cannot catch you, the perilous pestilence (that is, deadly diseases of epidemic proportions—not just what destroys food crops) cannot find you, the darts of the enemy cannot reach you, and no night terrors can locate you. You are, indeed, off the grid. Untouchable; literally "kept by the power of God through faith." (1 Peter 1:5)

The present-day deliverance ministry of Jesus Christ is not only to cast out the demonic, as important as that is, but to draw us into a hidden state in Him where the lion and the cobra cannot find us.

What this book aims to do is give some insight on how to reach that place in Jesus. I have most definitely not attained, and very few people I know have either, but that does not negate the principle of truth that we can live above the Snake Line. Like Paul, I want to, "...press toward the goal for the prize of the upward call of God in Christ Jesus." (Philippians 3:14)

With God's grace, perhaps this book can help us both toward that goal line, or rather, Snake Line.

Dwelling in the Secret Place

Back to Psalm 91, we have most likely heard numerous teachings on "the secret place." This is not just an abstract concept. Some ideal that leads to a better quality of life, but rather, it is a literal place that can only be spiritually perceived. Just as heaven and hell are real places, not conceptual notions, the secret place is a literal state of being. My point is, there is a place of residency in your walk with God that you can arrive at wherein all of the promises outlined in the rest of the psalm become your portion—provided you *dwell* in that place. The total and complete protection of the secret place is conditional upon your remaining there. You cannot leave it. When you venture down off the mountain, you'll face snakes and lions, but if you live—*abide*—in the secret place of the Most High, you're invulnerable and unassailable.

The Hebrew word for "dwell" (Strong's #3427) most properly means "to sit down," and conveys the notion of lying quietly in wait. To hide out. It means to inhabit a place, to tarry in that location, to be set somewhere and to remain there indefinitely, to make an abode and continue living there. The word carries a sense of permanence, not transience. It is often translated "still" as in sit still, tarry still, be still, remain still. The opposite of moving around.

"Secret place" in the Hebrew (Strong's #5643) is an interesting word. It is sometimes translated as a "cover or covering" literally or figuratively—something "covert," as in Psalm 61:4. It means a shelter, a place of protection against the elements. With a negative connotation, it is translated in one verse of Job as a "disguise" for the face; once as "privily" (in private) in Psalm 101; and once is used in Proverbs for a "backbiting tongue," that is to speak slanderously in secret.

The idea of a secret place is a place of hiding. The root of the word means to conceal carefully, to cover up—to hide by covering, to be kept close; to be absent, not there in the place of danger, but somewhere else protectively and thoroughly concealed from sight.

"Abide" in this instance implies to "stay permanently," and the root of it, interestingly enough, means to be tenaciously obstinate—that is, stubborn and determined, which is why sometimes the word is translated "murmur" when used with a negative connotation: to complain pig-headedly, to grumble and hold a grudge. In Psalm 91, it means to dig your heels in mulishly and remain adamantly, inflexibly unmoved, to abide permanently in the place you are set. A modern explanation would be "rooted in concrete."

"Shadow" comes from the Hebrew word meaning "to sink or submerge" or "to grow dark or opaque"—in this instance, opaque means impervious, impenetrable, solid, obscured and dense, the opposite of transparent. It also means twilight, falling shade, through the idea of the Most High hovering over us, casting His shadow upon us. We are swallowed up by His great shadow, and therefore nothing can perceive us because we are utterly hidden by Him. It can be compared to another Hebrew word meaning to cast an "image" over something, to shade.

Can you believe all of this comes from just the first verse of Psalm 91? That's why it's such a potent passage of scripture. "He who dwells in the secret place of the Most High shall abide under the shadow of the Almighty." The word Almighty refers to deity obviously. It is where *El-Shaddai* comes from, God Most Powerful. Of interesting note, the root means "to be burly" or passively "impregnably powerful" and actually implies the ability to "destroy utterly, devastate, despoil, assault violently and lay waste to." The point here is, we are to abide under the shadow of One who has the power to crush and destroy everything in His path, even the works of the lions and the snakes.

We're not just clinging to the apron strings of a mediocre person here. No, the Lord's brawny bulkiness is casting a long, dark shadow over us as He fills the entire sky, showing Himself capable of violently wrecking the activities of those who would mean us harm.

Juxtapose that to the beautiful imagery of being softly covered over with His feathers as we take refuge under His colossal, all-powerful wings. "Under His wings" (Verse 4) means we are shielded by God's presence; think of them as a bubble of protection, a force field that covers over you completely.

To refer to Spurgeon again, he called it "transcendent condescension," that had it come from any other source, it would border on blasphemy—to akin Almighty God to a bird. And yet the composer of the psalm, still under the inspiration of the

Spirit, turns the phrasing again by saying the truth of God—that is His firmness, stability, faithfulness, sureness, reliability (see Strong's #571)—shall be our shield and buckler.

Those are two different things. "Shield" comes from a root meaning "to be prickly" like a thorn or barb, a hook, a cactus hedge—or the piercing cold of stinging snow, or cooling refreshment (see Strong's #6791), and it describes a large shield that covers the entire body. (Strong's #6793) The Hebrew word translated "buckler" is only used in this one verse, and it means "shield" too, but with the concept of surrounding, defending, like a tower or fortress. The root means "to go around" and was used to describe the traffic of merchants who traded their wares here, there, and everywhere. So again, the connotation is defended completely from all angles—not by one means of armor, but two! Double protection; in other words, fully covered.

And at all times: by night and by day, in darkness and at high noon—because His shadow is all-encompassing. The sun in its incessant circuit from east to west will never dispel the immeasurable shadow cast by God's "bigness." Everyone else not abiding under His wings is subject to terror, disease, flying weapons and destruction—a thousand, ten thousand may fall, but you won't. None of those things can touch you, because you are hidden in Him.

"'No weapon formed against you shall prosper, and every tongue which rises against you in judgment you shall condemn. This is the heritage of the servants of the Lord, and their righteousness is from Me,' says the Lord." (Isaiah 54:17)

"Terror by night" (Verse 5) speaks about a clandestine invasion catching you unawares. Our sleep is sweet to us because we know we are being watched over by the Lord in the night hours. He never slumbers and He is never caught off guard by a covert operation of the enemy. Even while you are sleeping, His never-tiring eyes are watching over you, and He is replenishing your strength.

"When you lie down, you will not be afraid; yes, you will lie down and your sleep will be sweet." (Proverbs 3:24)

"'For I have satiated the weary soul, and I have replenished every sorrowful soul.' After this I awoke and looked around, and my sleep was sweet to me." (Jeremiah 31:25-26)

The "arrow that flies by day" means that even as you go about your daily business—at work, at home, taking care of your children, grocery shopping, in the shower, on the phone, or in your car—the Lord will not permit a "rocket attack" from some hidden enemy to strike you. He keeps the enemy so far away, their only recourse is to launch missiles at you; and even then, as we abide in Him, these arrows miss their mark and fall harmlessly to the ground.

We are protected even from the shrapnel of the enemy's attacks in our daily encounters with the people around us. Sadly, those who aren't abiding in Him are subject to these booby traps—a thousand, *ten* thousand may be affected, "but it shall not come near you." (Verse 7) This speaks of a supernatural shield that covers over you, so even when "the pestilence that walks in darkness" (Verse 6) strikes from the dark recesses of human society—theologians equate this to epidemic disease or germ warfare—you are protected.

Theologians have taught that the "destruction that lays waste at noonday" speaks of calamity on a global level, something that is capable of causing ten thousand to fall in one fell swoop. We could equate this to something akin to nuclear fallout. Your protection in Him is so complete, you need not fear even an atomic attack!

As we abide in Him, we are fully protected from the traps and wiles of our enemy. The phrase in Psalm 91:3 is literally, "one who catches birds in a trap."

"Refuge" (Verse 9) is shelter from storms and also shelter from falsehood—you are kept from falling into deceit and being tricked. (Strong's #4268) Its root means to flee for protection, to put your trust and hope in Someone who will watch over you— the Person to whom one runs for protection. "Dwelling place" or "habitation" is a home, a lair, a den, a retreat, an asylum. (Strong's #4583) The root is only used once in the Old Testament, and it refers to marriage duties, dwelling together as husband and wife; conjugal rights, not to put too fine a point on it.

God Himself, your great King and Husband, has charged His servants, the heavenly host—all of them!—to guard you carefully and protect you completely. To walk with you, arm in arm, guiding you so you don't trip and fall. Yes, so you don't so much as stub your toe! (Strong's #5062) That's careful supervision.

You are so kept by Him that even the roving, ravenous plagues—diseases of the body that consume the flesh—will not be able to approach your dwelling. (Verse 10) The Hebrew word there implies even the marks of disease and is elsewhere translated as "sores, strokes, wounds, stripes." (Strong's #5061)

Your very house is kept free and clear from pandemic afflictions. The physical place you live (literally, your "tent," Strong's #168) becomes a shelter when you abide in the shadow of the Almighty, and no evil will befall you.

That word "evil" encompasses afflictions, mischief, troubles, wickedness, unhappiness, miseries, harm, griefs, malignancy, distresses, adversities, injuries, wretchedness, wrongs, vexations, being ill-favored. (Strong's #7451)

The word "befall" is related to "sighing or groaning, lamenting, mourning," to contract oneself in anguish. (Strong's #578; #579) Rather than bewailing our plights, we will be treading upon them.

The primitive root for "tread" (Verse 13) means to march upon and trample down. (Strong's #1869) In one place it is translated "thresh." (Jeremiah 51:33) Now, I also find it interesting the word is used to mean "stringing a bow" because the archer bent the bow to string it by treading on it. So there is a martial act to "treading upon the lion and the cobra": archers marching and stringing their bows.

"Lion" and "young lion" probably don't need a translation—"lion" means something that roars. That's deep. Theologians have equated that first lion to be the counterfeit of the Lion of Judah—the devil pretending to be something he is not, more powerful than he truly is. See 1 Peter 5:8. That is who we will trample upon.

I also want to point out "young lion" (the root of which comes from being "covered"—as with a mane—or pitched, and is where the concept of covering sin through a propitiation or atonement comes from; see Strong's #3722) means a weaned lion, in the prime of youth, who has learned to devour man. And as an aside, the word also means "village," a place that is covered, protected, because of its walls. So, one could argue we shall tread down walls.

"Cobra," or "adder" in the KJV, is a poisonous snake obviously, but the root word means to contort or twist around, as a snake does. The KJV translates "serpent" as "dragon." And while that may sound like just poetic usage, the word does mean a sea monster, perhaps a plesiosaur—though it is sometimes translated "jackal" or "whale." The root means something "elongated" and carries the connotation of something preternaturally formed. That means "a monster," either from the depths of the sea or a kind of wolflike wild dog. We're talking about something more hideous than a simple garter snake here.

Regardless, all these nasty things will be trampled under our feet. The primitive root of this word comes from a potter treading clay with his feet—it means to "stamp down on," and can signify one oppressing another, holding them "under their feet." The point here is that all of these monstrous things are not supposed to tyrannize and afflict us, *we* are to dominate *them*, that is "stomp them down."

Why shall we be able to do this, to live in a state of repressing and subjugating our enemies? Because we have set our love upon the Lord. That phrase means most properly because we have "joined ourselves" with God. (Strong's #2836) Because we "cling and cleave" to Him and are "delighted" to be so close to Him, He will deliver us.

"Deliver" means "to slip away." (Strong's #6403) It properly means to be "smooth and sleek," and speaks of calving, or sliding from the womb.

Our Lord will set us on high; that is to say, He takes us to a place so "lofty," we are inaccessibly high, out of reach, and cannot be captured.

The second use of "deliver" (Strong's #2502) in Verse 15 is another word, and this one means "to draw out, remove, withdraw;" but also means "to equip for war, to arm soldiers." And in Isaiah 58:11 (KJV) it is translated "make fat thy bones," for indeed when it says God will "honor" us, that means "make us heavy." Not physically heavy, thankfully! But weighty, of substance and worth.

The Lord promises to "satiate us with many days" and show us His salvation. That's the word *yeshua* (Strong's #3444), the root of which properly means "to be wide open, spacious, free," and figuratively "opulently ample." It carries the connotation of not only being rescued, preserved, defended, delivered, liberated and succored, but also victoriously avenged.

All of that from sixteen verses! This is what it truly means to live above the Snake Line! In order to do so more fully, let's take a bit and look at how we can arrive this secret place: the key word is *deliverance*.

No, not the Johnny Cash number; I mean "walking the Line" is to be a way of life. Deliverance is a perpetual path that is to encompass every facet of our personal existence: spirit, soul and body. The present-day deliverance ministry of Jesus Christ is not just a singular occurrence that takes place the moment we are born again. Rather, that is just the start of a lifelong journey to free ourselves of things that keep us off the Line. Deliverance isn't just against the unclean spirits of satanic forces, but it is also freedom from ubiquitous sin and the natural "self," which is a much tougher enemy than our defeated foe.

"Therefore we also, since we are surrounded by so great a cloud of witnesses, let us lay aside every weight, and the sin which so easily ensnares us, and let us run with endurance the race that is set before us, looking unto Jesus, the author and finisher of our faith, who for the joy that was set before Him endured the cross, despising the shame, and has sat down at the right hand of the throne of God." (Hebrews 12:1-2)

God's purpose is that His children are to be delivered wholly from the old creation they were first born into, entering fully into the "new man." (Ephesians 4:24; Colossians 3:10)

"Do not remember the former things, nor consider the things of old. Behold, I will do a new thing, now it shall spring forth; shall you not know it? I will even make a road in the wilderness and rivers in the desert. The beast of the field will honor Me, the jackals and the ostriches, because I give waters in the wilderness and rivers in the desert, to give drink to My people, My chosen. This people I have formed for Myself; they shall declare My praise." (Isaiah 43:18-21)

We are to receive Jesus' power of deliverance down into the depths of our whole being, not only in the spirit man, but out through the mind and emotions, even in the determination of our will, expressing this freedom through our physical bodies. All of us are to be fashioned after Christ, and while this life process starts out beset with trials, suffering and failures—it will not need to be this way always! The concepts in this book will prayerfully build on what the Lord is already teaching you, and in due order, you and I both can walk the Line perfectly.

"...Precept upon precept, precept upon precept, line upon line, line upon line, here a little, there a little..." (Isaiah 28:13)

Because of this, this book is not necessarily written to convince someone they need to find the path to the Snake Line, but rather for those who are *already* seeking to know the way. To benefit the most from this material, you must already have a personal need, a desire to walk in a lifestyle of deliverance. I'm not going to spend a hundred pages trying to convince you of this, as it's not my job in the first place. Let the Spirit induce you to find the secret place, "...finding out what is acceptable to the Lord," (Ephesians 5:10), and I will pray that this book helps you along the way.

And a quick word of caution: guard yourself against excessive self-analyzation as you read this book. I'm going to be outlining a lot of "nasty things" that the general body of Christ might need to deal with—not necessarily *you* in every case. If you dissect yourself minutely, without the Spirit prompting and guiding you in love to do so, you can fall into the trap of getting your eyes off Christ and onto yourself—which is another thing that can keep you from the Snake Line.

To the degree we keep our focus on Him is the degree to which we are delivered from ourselves. I think someone much smarter than myself said that once, but I can't recall who it was.

But on the other side of the coin, don't fall into the deception that you have this whole deliverance thing down pat and, therefore, the following doesn't apply to you. We all have areas that need to be swept clean—it is the Holy Spirit's job to bring it to your attention, little by little, always gently leading, never cracking you over the head with a hickory stick. The idea of this book is to be set free, not shackled to a "Boy, you and I are a sorry lot, aren't we?" frame of mind.

First Thessalonians 5:23 tells us we are comprised of a threefold existence: spirit, soul and body. Hebrews 4:12 shows the spirit, the soul, and the body are separate from each other; and since they can all be divided by the Word, they must be different in nature. The Old Testament illustration of the priest using a sword to dissect completely the sacrifice is appropriate in showing that nothing "inside" can be hidden. The Lord uses the Word in like fashion to separate us thoroughly into our three components of existence, dividing the soul from the spirit from the body.

Our life itself comes from the Spirit (John 6:63) and entered into our "dust bodies" when God breathed in His breath of life, according to Genesis 2:7. Romans 8:16 shows the distinction between *the* Spirit and *our* spirit—they are separate entities, one receiving its life from the Other. (For more biblical references of the distinction of the human spirit, see Proverbs 25:28; Zechariah 12:1; 1 Corinthians 2:11; 5:4; 14:14; 14:32; Hebrews 12:23.)

The soul (mind, will and emotions) was created when the spirit reacted with the body, a combination of both, which forms a unique individual. This book deals primarily with the soul, because it is the organ of man's freewill. If a person's soul wills to obey God, the spirit is then allowed to rule over one's life as He intended.

"Do you not know that you are the temple of God and that the Spirit of God dwells in you?" (1 Corinthians 3:16)

The Old Testament temple was divided into three parts forming a whole: the outer court is one's physical body, seen by all, lit by daylight; the holy place represents the soul, wherein we as priests approach God by offering our sacrifice, and is lit by candlelight, shown only to those whom we wish to see our thoughts and emotions; and the most holy place wherein His very Presence resides, lit by Himself as *the* Light. We commune with the Lord in our spirits, the holiest part of our existence. (John 4:24)

The soul is the center for a person's rational thoughts, their knowledge of the material world. It is in this place that we must walk the Line of deliverance in order to ensure our spirit man controls the soul by revelation found only in the Holy of Holies.

The spirit is to have preeminence in all of the functions of our souls and bodies. The present-day deliverance ministry of Jesus Christ is the means by which we can do this.

Now remember, this is speaking of our current, natural existence. The soul is presently the meeting point of the other two areas of our existence, but in our resurrection state, the spirit will be the prime component. (1 Corinthians 15:44)

The exciting news, though, is that since we have been united to the resurrected Lord, our spirits can rule in the *now* over our beings. We are not united to the first Adam, but to the last Adam, who is a life-giving Spirit. (1 Corinthians 14:45)

The body is the means of world-consciousness, that is, the five senses. The soul is the means of the intellect, the "self," the personality. The spirit is the means of communication with God, because He dwells there once we are born again. So while the body communicates with the material world, and the spirit communicates with the spiritual world, the soul is the midway point, so to speak, between the two—it is exposed to both worlds. But the spirit cannot act upon the body directly and must go through the soul. So the spirit transmits the thoughts and directives of God to the soul, the soul in turn transmits this to the body, so that the body can obey the spirit's order.

Does this make sense? It might sound a little convoluted, since most people think of the soul and the spirit as the same entity, but once you understand the distinction, the above isn't that hard to grasp.

God's great plan, therefore, is for the spirit to govern and subdue the body by the means of the soul. It is in this way that His light shines forth to the world at large, and yet we still remain ourselves at the same time, with a uniquely expressive personality.

We must be well acquainted with our spirits, for that is where communication between God and man occurs. If we are ignorant of this existence, it's easy to get confused between the thoughts and emotions of the soul, substituting those as "words from God."

Further, there is a difference between the conscience of the soul (knowing right from wrong) and knowledge the brain has acquired physically. Conscience is an extemporaneous judgment based on reasoning within ourselves—"this is right, or this is wrong." This is how people can justify sin in their particular circumstance even while *knowing* it's wrong because they have read the Bible that tells them so.

Intuition, on the other hand, is different from conscience. It is a spiritual faculty that is not dependent on any outside influence; we don't get any help from the soul. We just "know that we know" something. You know you're born again. How? Intuitively. We *know* through intuition, but our mind helps us *understand* what we know. All of God's revelation, and the moving of His Spirit, are perceived through intuition.

These two faculties, conscience and intuition, are not competent in their own right to commune with God (worship)—this only occurs directly Spirit to spirit.

Conscience judges according to intuition, and intuition is connected to communion in that God is known by it, and thus, worshipped in response. Because what else do you do with God, once you know Him, but worship Him? That's the point of God's existence: to be worshipped.

The point of all this is to show the importance of the soul as it relates to the spirit and the body. Nearly every aspect of "battle" you will have against the enemy is in the soulish life, and that which takes place in the realm of the body in the name of sickness or disease most often (say, 95% of the time) has some link to the soulish realm. When you are born again, the battle for your spirit is already won. But in this natural life, all that you possess, all that you are, all that you may become is determined in the realm of the soul. The overwhelming majority of the present-day deliverance ministry of Jesus Christ, then, takes place in the soul.

The word *flesh* has different meanings, apart from just meaning the physical body. One of them is the "old you," referring to the fallen nature. In an unregenerate state, the spirit is dead toward God and, therefore, a person is wholly dominated by soul and body. When Adam's soul resisted his spirit's authority, it was sold to the desires of the body. This created a pattern in which the soul leans (this is called *iniquity*) to the body instead of the spirit—the soul was made a prisoner to the body when Adam's will resisted God's rule. When the soul is under the power of flesh, we are carnally ruled.

Now, there are two types of born again Christians: spiritual and carnal. The spirit itself is perfected at salvation—the new life is finalized, but it is waiting to be matured. Just as in the natural, a new birth cannot instantly be full grown. The life in a flower may be perfect in order to turn into fruit, but the fruit is still unripe. It takes time to grow, and your will plays the most significant role in how fast you grow.

A spiritual Christian is one in whom the Holy Spirit has become so preeminent He controls the entire being. Very few, if any, of us are at this completed stage yet—but it *is* possible to achieve by yielding to the Spirit's help. To the level our carnality is subjugated, this is the level to which we can achieve living above the Snake Line.

A carnal Christian is one whose spirit has been brought to life by *the* Spirit, but still submits to his or her soul and body in sin at certain instances. And there are levels of carnality. To the level in which our carnality is not put to death, this is the level to which the enemy can keep us from living above the Snake Line.

"For to be carnally minded is death, but to be spiritually minded is life and peace... For if you live according to the flesh you will die; but if by the Spirit you put to death the deeds of the body, you will live." (Romans 8:6,13)

Praise God, He has provided—through the death of Jesus, by the help of the Holy Spirit—full salvation, complete victory, over the "old you"! It is in this way we can walk the Line to the Highway of Holiness.

"A highway shall be there, and a road,
And it shall be called the Highway of Holiness.
The unclean shall not pass over it,
But it shall be for others.
Whoever walks the road, although a fool,
Shall not go astray.
No lion shall be there,
Nor shall any ravenous beast go up on it;
It shall not be found there.
But the redeemed shall walk there,
And the ransomed of the Lord shall return,
And come to Zion with singing,
With everlasting joy on their heads.
They shall obtain joy and gladness,
And sorrow and sighing shall flee away.

—Isaiah 35:8-10

3

The Highway of Holiness

ebrews 4:9 says, "There remains therefore a rest for the people of God," and I believe this is talking about the "secret place"—yes, there is a *place* in God that is very safe—where there is rest from the turmoil of life and the vexation of the enemy cannot find you. There is a *position* that we can place ourselves in where we live above the Snake Line.

I do not believe it is supposed to be the position of God's people to live under constant attacks of the enemy, under a heavy sense of doom and gloom. While I do not teach that *everything* goes our way, every day of our lives, I am convinced that there is a secret place, a position in Christ, a "high mountainous area" where the enemy cannot approach. The intent of this book is to present a challenge to "come up higher" in God. Living above the Snake Line is living above the realm of relentless assaults.

In truth, we fight to maintain our confidence more than fight with the enemy; but I mean, if everyone fights with the "beasts of Ephesus" (1 Corinthians 15:32) on a weekly basis, are we really living the abundant life? (See John 10:10.)

"Now it shall come to pass in the latter days that the mountain of the Lord's house shall be established on the top of the mountains, and shall be exalted above the hills; and peoples shall flow to it. Many nations shall come and say, 'Come, and let us go up to the mountain of the Lord, to the house of the God of Jacob; He will teach us His ways, and we shall walk in His paths.' For out of Zion the law shall go forth, and the word of the Lord from Jerusalem." (Micah 4:1-2)

If we get to the point where we are living on the mountain of the Lord, it will draw others to come with us. "Let us go up to the mountain... we shall walk in His paths." How exciting a notion!

Ephesians 2:6 tells us we are seated together in "heavenly places" with Jesus. And yet, for many of us—and I speak to myself as much as to you, dear reader—this path to the Lord's mountain seems far off, some future place we can get to if we trudge through the wilderness and fight off monsters along the way.

I remain convinced this is to be a way of life in the present. We must find this path—this way to walk in God wherein the devil may not pass by. Such a path *does* exist!

"That path no bird knows, nor has the falcon's eye seen it. The proud lions have not trodden it, nor has the fierce lion passed over it." (Job 28:7-8)

This path, the enemy cannot perceive it; the vulture's eye (see KJV) has never even seen it. It's a path—a walkway on the journey through life—hidden with Christ in God (again, Colossians 3:3.) In Colossians 2:3, referring to Christ, it says, "in whom are hidden all the treasures of wisdom and knowledge." Therefore, it is "in Him" that we find this path. This speaks of a *joining*—we are being "put to death" after a fashion by connecting ourselves with Christ, hiding ourselves in His life (since we have forfeited our own to Him anyway); and this hidden life in Him cannot be seen by Satan and his demons. This is supposed to be the life of every believer!

There is a Highway of Holiness (Isaiah 35:8) leading to the secret place of hiding in God. What will be true on the physical earth during His literal reign is true in the "new creation" spiritually right now. But of course, the unclean shall not pass over it. Just as no ravenous beast or lion can tread there, neither can the unjust.

The clause "although a fool" should not be taken as a permissive stance on the Lord's part to allow immorality to go unchecked. That word means one who "despises wisdom, mocks when guilty, quarrelsome and licentious" (Strong's #191)—basically an impious person. Of course there is grace in the Lord, forgiveness and restoration; but let us not forget other verses that speak of fools: Psalm 107:17; Proverbs 10:8; 10:14; 10:21; 14:9; 16:22; 29:9. The point here is, we should not be *remaining* fools and expect to stay on the Highway of Holiness leading to the secret place.

This tells me that we need to have a heart-searching attitude to uproot anything that is not consecrated (declared "holy") unto God. While we're hiding out under the shadow of the Almighty, we're not supposed to be sleeping there. The "rest" of God is actually a state of occupation—actively waiting, not just kicking back and sipping iced tea. We're supposed to be wakeful and vigilant, not just of the enemy *out there*, but giving no place to the enemy *in here*.

And this is a form of deliverance—not everything is a demon that needs to be cast out. I wish it were that simple. Honestly, one of the easiest aspects of this book is the actual deliverance part itself. The real difficulty lies in dealing with *ourselves*. Sin must be confessed and turned away from. You and I can not get around this. Our flesh needs to be continually crucified with Christ in "death," so that we might remain hidden in Him. Our flesh will give away our position to the enemy every time, and eventually those ravenous beasts will catch our scent and come to take a nibble. Unconfessed sin gives off the stench of carrion rot and decay that will draw every predator for miles around.

Walking by Faith

But how exactly—for those of us who are putting down our foolish natures—are we to remain on this path? "For we walk by faith, not by sight." (2 Corinthians 5:7) This is a spiritual path that requires a spiritual walk; our natural perceptions and circumstances are subject to our footsteps of faith. We all know that without faith it is impossible to please God. (Hebrews 11:6) Just so, the path to His mountain is taken by faith.

You have probably heard it taught that faith is active; it is not trust, which is passive. The only way to take a step of faith is to... take a step of faith. Now that may seem glib, but the passage from Micah says, "Come and let us go..." There is a decision on our parts to make this trek.

One of the areas of deliverance necessary to live above the Snake Line is exercising our God-given authority over the enemy who is trying to enervate us.

"He shall speak pompous words against the Most High, shall persecute the saints of the Most High, and shall intend to change times and law. Then the saints shall be given into his hand for a time and times and half a time." (Daniel 7:25)

That word *persecute* means literally "wear out." This is one of the major tactics of the devil, to wear you out to the point of exhaustion so that you *can't* take a step of faith on the pathway to God's mountain. That's not to say we all don't have times of tiredness and fatigue. Even the Lord was tired sometimes while on this earth. (See John 4:6.) But notice His response—He withdrew into the "secret place" of His Father's mountain. (See Matthew 14:13; Mark 1:35; Luke 6:12.)

There is a rest for the people of God. Sadly, many of us miss it, because we don't perceive by faith and stay on the pathway to the high place of God.

"For with stammering lips and another tongue He will speak to this people, to whom He said, 'This is the rest with which You may cause the weary to rest,' and, 'This is the refreshing'; yet they would not hear." (Isaiah 28:11-12)

I have heard it taught that this word "rest" in the Greek, which is discussed at length in Hebrews 4, is where we get our English word "catapult." (See Strong's #2663.) The connotation, then, is that this rest is the means by which the strongholds (see the next chapter) of the mind and emotions are cast down from their high and lofty positions.

This "rest" is found in the stammering lips and another tongue. It is by the willful "lending" of our tongue to the indwelling Holy Spirit, praying in our heavenly language, whereby we enter into His rest and are refreshed. So terribly sad, then, that people of God in this day would not hear of it, by rejecting the importance of speaking in tongues, but this is not going to be us!

While we are finding that path toward this rest, the enemy is going to do what it can to pester us to the point of exhaustion. But we need to be like Paul. Every time a snake lunges out, shake it off into the fire! (See Acts 28.) We cannot forget that while we are taking the steps of faith upon the pathway, we do not go alone. The Holy Spirit has equipped us to exercise authority in every circumstance the enemy brings against us.

Nevertheless, it is faith that activates that same authority. Paul *knew* the viper wouldn't harm him; you can't convince me otherwise. It was never the Lord's intention that a recipient of the Spirit become an expert in the realm of the movings of that same Spirit, yet remain a novice in the realm of faith. They work hand in hand. See, because the movings of the Spirit bless us, we are prone to live by feeling, rather than faith. And yet it is our faith that pleases God.

"Nevertheless, when the Son of Man comes, will He really find faith on the earth?" (Luke 18:8)

Good question. When Jesus returns, will He find people

41

exercising their faith to overcome? Here's a good one-liner: "God isn't so much concerned with the emotionally unstable Christian as He is with the unbelief in the stable one." (Dr. Roy H. Hicks, Sr.)

"For whatever is born of God overcomes the world. And this is the victory that has overcome the world—our faith... These things I have written to you who believe in the name of the Son of God, that you may know that you have eternal life, and that you may continue to believe in the name of the Son of God." (1 John 5:4,13)

Applying Christ's Victory

It is by faith that we apply Christ's total victory over the enemy. We know that He completely conquered Satan at the cross, but *we* must enforce it.

Some of the following principles have been adapted from teachings given by my late brother-in-law, David Alsobrook, and are used here with permission.

Psalm 8 states that God made us to have dominion over the works of His hands and put all things under our feet. (Verse 6) Hebrews 2:8 makes it clear that we don't see all things put under our feet right now, but we *do* see Jesus, who was crowned with glory and honor because He "tasted death for everyone." Everything is under Jesus—He is Lord over all!

"...Which He worked in Christ when He raised Him from the dead and seated Him at His right hand in the heavenly places, far above all principality and power and might and dominion, and every name that is named, not only in this age but also in that which is to come." (Ephesians 1:20-21)

Of course we know Satan is the prince of this world system (again, Ephesians 2:2), but Jesus' victory over him at the cross ruined, disarmed, spoiled all of his abilities and left him in utter humiliation. Nothing more has to be done for sin, but the question is, how much victory do you want? We need to enjoy the full victory that Christ provided, and that requires our application of His victory in all areas of life, not just the remission of sins.

Why are so many of Jesus' followers under the devil's influence? If Jesus destroyed Satan's works, (again, that's 1 John 3:8) why do believers succumb to his works? Christ came so that we could have a more abundant life in *this* life. (And again, John 10:10.)

I'm not speaking of biblical sufferings—the persecutions and distresses of being connected to Christ. I'm talking about Christians who labor under continual, or habitual, sin issues, sicknesses, anxiety, fears, worries, woes. These things were taken out of operational existence by the cross. I think the majority of us would qualify for the statement that we need to enjoy the victory of Christ in a fuller degree.

Where is that victory? There seems to be a great discrepancy for a wide section of the body of Christ wherein what we *possess* is much lower than what we *profess*. And let's be real frank, defeated Christians can become a stumbling block for other Christians and the world at large. We don't want this!

Now look, like I said in the first chapter, I'm not cudgeling anyone here, just being candid. I know that there are many, many Christians who do live in that kind of victory, those who live in a perpetual state of overcoming, even while not always totally euphoric with joy. Those who, excepting some shortcomings few and far between, are living a life of overall triumph. But if we were to be quite honest with ourselves, most of us don't fall into this category.

Let's look at some keys that we can apply to help this. I don't claim to have all the answers, but this book is attempting to outline a few means by which we can move toward that Snake Line in our walk with God.

Matthew 16:19 talks about keys of the kingdom—binding and loosing. A lot of books on deliverance talk about the binding part, and rightfully so, but I think the loosing is just as important. We are to have a love of Jesus that is so possessing, so utterly consuming, so intensely overshadowing that we are experiencing a loosing of His Spirit at all times in every facet of our lives, from the mundane to the monumental. Keeping ourselves glued to the Lord, so to speak. Saying no to self and yes to God at all times. Many Christians are not fully alive to God because they are not dead to self.

This is what Hebrews 12:16 is talking about: a "profane person like Esau." When self is ruling, even partly, much grace and power is of necessity withdrawn—or rather, you move away from that positioning of available grace, allowing the enemy to come in seemingly like a flood.

But the better news is, when we reverentially fear the Lord and honor Him, versus honoring ourselves, the Bible tells us He will raise His standard against the enemy on our behalves.

"So shall they fear the name of the Lord from the west, and His glory from the rising of the sun; when the enemy comes in like a flood, the Spirit of the Lord will lift up a standard against him." (Isaiah 59:19)

This is why James 4:7 tells us, "Therefore submit to God. Resist the devil and he will flee from you."

That word "submit" (Strong's #5293) is a Greek military term meaning to arrange troops under the command of a leader. It speaks of being disciplined, moving in a militaristic, soldiery fashion, like troops being marshaled under one ruler, moving as a cohesive unit. Obedience stemming from discipline. Soldiers drill and drill to make sure they execute the commands of their leader, so that when the enemy rises against them, they respond immediately and appropriately to put the attackers to flight. The anonymous adage, "The more you sweat in practice, the less you bleed in battle," is fitting here.

It has been taught elsewhere that submitting oneself voluntarily under the rule of God could be phrased, "Show forth your discipline." To come under the mighty hand of the Lord and be directed by Him. In other words, act like a solider would act, marching in time to the commands of the Lord with a martial discipline. This doesn't happen overnight; one must practice and practice so that these responses become second nature. Without even thinking, the good soldier responds to the threat of an enemy correctly and instantaneously. Their disciplined training has been so ingrained in their actions that it is an auto-response.

"Submit" means to know yourself like you know the back of your own hand. You get to a place where you know the Lord's command before He even speaks it—you *think* like He thinks. So when the enemy rises against you, you already *know* the proper way to resist him. Thus, he is set to rout.

So if you find yourself saying, "I'm going through a time here where the enemy seems to be winning, and all of my rebukes in Jesus' name don't seem to be working. What do I do?", it would probably serve better to ask yourself, "Where have I missed showing forth my discipline? Where have I been unsubmitted to the Lord?" And remember, it's little foxes that spoil the vines. (Song of Solomon 2:15) (I don't think *unsubmitted* is a real word, but you know what I mean.)

Most of us aren't in wanton, egregious sin—it's against our born-again nature to do so. But nevertheless, I believe just about everyone of us, if we were to really allow the Spirit to speak, would come to recognize those "little foxes" that we've been ignoring far too long.

But hey, the good news here is that all we need is more of Jesus' love to be shed abroad in our hearts. (Romans 5:5) Don't take that for a trite answer. It's a powerful truth that opens the door to deliverance and sets us on the path to the secret place.

Receiving Jesus' love frequently, and *in reality* (as with the Beloved, see John 13:23), changes us from the inside out. It's more than just a casual statement—"Oh, Jesus, I love you!" Rather, I'm speaking about entering into Him, His Person, leaning against His bosom with our full hearts, with no shame, no embarrassment, no reservation.

I've talked about "hug therapy" in other books. This is a spiritual truth, not an abstract vagary. We may be legally *in Him*, but experientially—well, there's a therapy that a lot of God's people aren't experiencing. Truthfully, there are many born again Christians who are not really experiencing His presence, who are not availing themselves as John did to the manifest presence of God. There is a blending, a union, with our Lord that only comes from experiencing His presence in our five senses.

"But he who is joined to the Lord is one spirit with Him." (1 Corinthians 6:17)

It's that kind of intimacy that sets us above the Snake Line. I think we all need to avail ourselves more of this "leaning" because the enemy cannot stand the presence of God.

"Let God arise, let His enemies be scattered; let those also who hate Him flee before Him." (Psalm 68:1)

There is a real truth that many of us overlook or downplay in seeking intimacy with our Lord, and that is found in praise and worship.

"But You are holy, enthroned in the praises of Israel." (Psalm 22:3)

I don't mean singing songs on Sunday morning only. I'm talking about the high praises of God in our mouths. (Psalm 149:6) The inner man is strengthened when we are in deep praise and worship on a regular, consistent basis. If we don't have time to devote to this kind of praise and worship, we are frankly too busy, and we need to restructure our workflow—it's as simple as that. I'm not saying we all have to be like the Golden Candlestick (see *Ladies of Gold* if you don't know what I'm talking about) and devote six hours a day to high praise and worship. They were called to a specific function with a special anointing for it.

And praise and worship, just for the sake of praise and worship, can become religious and legalistic without the Spirit's leading. If we're just "logging hours," that's not real intimacy, the kind that leads us above the Snake Line. However, it is safe to say we all need to make time ministering to the Lord a higher priority across the board.

Further to this, submitting ourselves to an anointed ministry is important. Those who give out to others constantly need to take in from others frequently. Don't neglect gathering with other believers. (Hebrews 10:25)

Also, standing on the Word is vital to applying the victory of Christ in a fuller way. I'm disheartened when I see saints downplaying the significance of feeding on the Word, and it happens all too frequently. Groups of students graduating from Bible college who cannot even recite the books of the Bible. Does that even make sense? Yet it happens more often than we'd like to admit.

In this day of modern technology constantly feeding us distractions and our super busy schedules, it seems that the preeminence of reading the Bible and spending time waiting on the Lord has slipped. I'm not meaning to be hypercritical; I know we're all extremely busy, and there are many factors involved; but each of us should make it a priority to feed more on the Word and sit in the presence of the Lord.

We stake our claim in Christ's provisions by confessing the Word. How can this be unimportant? Saying the same thing God has said about any given subject we are confronted with by the evil one—this begins to change our circumstances to line up with the Bible.

Confession in the Greek is *homologeo* (Strong's #3670, "ha-ma-la-gay-oh"), and it is a compound word meaning "saying together" or "same speech." That is, saying the same thing as someone else. The scriptures are not just printed words—they are the thoughts of God that He "in-breathed" and "out-breathed"—that means, what He spoke through the writers—His complete thought on a particular subject pertaining to our daily life. Thus, we need to speak the same thing, because obviously it was important enough to Him to say it in the first place.

Lastly, another key to applying Christ's victory is to repent *quickly*. We will be kept in triumph longer if we confess sin immediately rather than if we harden our hearts. This is just logical sense.

"When I kept silent, my bones grew old through my groaning all the day long. For day and night Your hand was heavy upon me; my vitality was turned into the drought of summer. Selah. I acknowledged my sin to You, and my iniquity I have not hidden. I said, 'I will confess my transgressions to the Lord,' and You forgave the iniquity of my sin." (Psalm 32:3-5)

"...The way of transgressors is hard." (Proverbs 13:15) "...The rebellious dwell in a dry land." (Psalm 68:6) This is not the path to take to rise above the Snake Line. Be quick to confess and repent. We need to keep Jesus' easy yoke around our necks (Matthew 11:30), and our path to His mountain becomes increasingly bright! "But the path of the just is like the shining sun, that shines ever brighter unto the perfect day." (Proverbs 4:18) Our place and our position in Him become stronger.

These may all seem like extremely simple notions, and they are meant to be. That does not make them any less important. When we're harried by the enemy, we tend to look for the looming, explosive solutions to our problems, and we can sometimes miss the simple, "little" things that are actually powerful tools we've forgotten to utilize.

How much victory do you want? Sadly, most believers don't enjoy the full victory Christ provided for them. Nevertheless, you and I, as we proceed on this Highway of Holiness, need to affirm that we have manifested the victory of Jesus over the attacks of Satan. No matter how great the trial, or how hard the problem is, there is always an answer in God for victory.

And it is up to us to enforce that victory. It is a truth that Jesus completely defeated the devil—he is nothing today like he once was. He *is* a crushed foe. We cannot blame God; it is important we assume the responsibility here to enforce the victory Jesus won on our behalves. It bears repeating: the enemy has *already* been defeated permanently by One much greater than you!

So the devil really isn't our problem—we need to look

elsewhere for the cause of our defeats. We won't have more of Christ's victory if we have too much of *us*. The problem, then, is ourselves—the rise of "self" in our lives, giving open opportunities for the devil to exploit.

"Now thanks be to God who always leads us in triumph in Christ, and through us diffuses the fragrance of His knowledge in every place. For we are to God the fragrance of Christ among those who are being saved and among those who are perishing. To the one we are the aroma of death leading to death, and to the other the aroma of life leading to life. And who is sufficient for these things?" (2 Corinthians 2:14-16)

This passage is true. God *always* leads us in triumph—every time, without exception. He does this because it "diffuses the fragrance of His knowledge" to everyone else. Those of us giving off the fragrance of victory distinguish between those who are living and those who are perishing.

In other words, our victorious living will either bring people to Christ, or push them away. It is a confrontational experience that demands others to give a response. That is why it is so vitally important for us to live victoriously, to give off the "best scent" as it were.

Now, if we're not giving off this fragrance, it isn't God's fault, because again the verses above are one hundred percent true: He *always* leads us. It is time, then, for us to search ourselves, with the Spirit's help, and make sure the broken, paralyzed enemy hasn't found an easy inroad to push us off the Highway of Holiness.

"Where there is no revelation, the people cast off restraint..."

—Proverbs 29:18

4

Destroying Strongholds

n Proverbs 29:18, that word *revelation* means "prophetic vision." For us to remain on the path to the secret place, it takes the aggressive help of the Holy Spirit working alongside us—we cannot forge ahead on our own and expect the enemy not to find us out. This is why I am always so adamant on the importance of a Spirit-filled life, building ourselves up in faith by praying in the Spirit. (Jude 20) We must be activated in the prophetic spirit in order to perceive properly the spiritual steps we are to take in order to reach the Lord's mountain. One of the major reasons why Christians remain under constant harassment is because we are not habitually becoming familiar with the Spirit.

This can create strongholds in our minds, wills and emotions. I'll more fully define "strongholds" throughout this chapter, but for right now, I mean they are habits, cycles, patterns of thinking and behavior, that limit our walk in the Spirit and hinder us from remaining hidden under the shadow of the Almighty.

In Ephesians 2:10, we are told to "walk in them" (the good works that God ordained for us.) That word *walk* in the Greek is *peripateo* ("pear-ee-pah-tay-oh," Strong's #4043); and it is comprised of the preposition *peri* (meaning "concerning, as touching, about, most properly *through*") and the verb *pateo*, which is derived from the root meaning "a path." So, that is to concern ourselves about the path we are treading upon.

We are supposed to be so habitually dependent on the Spirit as we walk, we could do it blindfolded because we know *He* is the one leading us along the way. Our natural eyes deceive us, and we stumble as we walk; but if the Spirit is guiding us, we won't trip.

This is opposed to "walking in the flesh." (Romans 8:1) Using our own perception and intuition—our own "pathfinding" abilities, as it were. In other words, our confidence isn't supposed to be in our own "flesh walk," but in the help of the Holy Spirit. He is the One who gives strategy, wisdom from above, where we are supposed to put our feet in order to avoid the traps and snares the enemy has laid before us.

Otherwise we might end up as the sons of Sceva. (See Acts 19:13-16.) If we are only concerned with the outward appearance of our walk—saying the "right things" but without the true power of the Spirit leading us along—well, our enemy is liable to say, "Jesus I know, Paul I know. Who are you?" We could be found on the path naked and wounded.

We cannot judge our walkway on the outward appearance: "This seems like the right way to go to me!" Without revelation, navigating our lives in a prophetic spirit that is being led by *the* Spirit, we can cast off restraint. We can get sidetracked down game trails that lead to the enemy's traps. It's foolish presumption to think we can direct our own steps, and that can lead to our falling down along the way.

Paul makes an excellent point in 2 Corinthians 11. The context is he recognizes the foolishness of operating "according to the flesh," and he fears "...lest somehow, as the serpent deceived Eve by his craftiness, so your minds may be corrupted from the simplicity that is in Christ. For if he who comes preaches another Jesus whom we have not preached, or if you receive a different spirit which you have not received, or a different gospel which you have not accepted—you may well put up with it!" (Verses 3-4)

He goes on to "boast" reluctantly that he is not inferior to other apostles (Verse 5), yet he humbled himself so that the disciples at Corinth might be exalted. (Verse 7) He does this to prove the invalidity of the false apostles, who have transformed themselves into apostles for Christ. (Verse 13) Much of the Book of Acts recounts the powerful miracles the Lord worked through Paul's hands. No one can question the man was a mighty apostle for Jesus.

But this goes along with the "not judging on outward appearance." Paul was base and unassuming. (2 Corinthians 10:1) Some scholars think, according to a second century document, he was a small-statured, uni-browed bald man. This is probably true; his Greek name *Paul* means "small, humble."

The point I wish to convey here is, Paul understood all too well the importance of "walking according to the Spirit" as the only way to avoid "putting up with" the enemy, who is very much capable of changing into an "angel of light." (Verse 14)

So the only way to live above the Snake Line is to be guided consistently by the revelation of the Spirit, to discern spiritually and not with our naked eye, the path we are to take.

Some of the problems we face when doing so are strongholds. At some point in our walk with the Lord, all of us will confront strongholds, and only the power of the Spirit Himself can eradicate them. We cannot surmount them in our own strength. This is why some people deal with the same issues that nag them, drag them down, for entire lifetimes. They do not press into the Spirit for revelation and the power to deal with what He reveals.

Think of strongholds like fortresses, buttresses, towers, great castles and citadels—areas in the battlefield of your mind, will and emotions (the soulish area of your existence) that are "forts" or "outposts" of the enemy stationed here and there to hamper and hinder your walk toward the mount of the Lord.

Strongholds are not demons themselves, but rather satanic ideologies and "doctrines"—ways of worldly thinking. They can be "mind-blinders," misconceptions you have about yourself and about God, perhaps areas of iniquity or unconfessed sin. I'm not badgering here; I think all of us have areas of our souls that need to be enlightened by the Spirit. But it doesn't change the fact that strongholds hinder the work of Jesus in your life.

A fortress is erected to keep outsiders from coming in. Perhaps you have been deeply wounded by someone in your past—most of us can think of at least one occurrence of this. Has the enemy raised a fortress around a part of your soul that keeps anyone from penetrating, even the light and love of the Spirit?

A prison is erected to keep someone inside from getting out. Has prior sin or iniquity kept you locked in a cell that you feel you can't escape from?

We're talking about places of detention—wherein you are held back from proceeding along the path—holding tanks that keep you locked up from entering the secret place of the Lord. These are strongholds. They exist to keep you in the earthly realm of your mind instead of perceiving the Spirit's revelation. James 3:15 says, "This wisdom does not descend from above, but is earthly, sensual, demonic."

This is Satan's strategy against you as you walk the Highway of Holiness: to build such strong lies in your mind so instead of being ruled by the Spirit, he can rule you from that high and lofty position in your thoughts and emotions. Whatever he can do to take away your peace. We know the enemy cannot touch our spirits, but he attempts to create thick, invisible walls that act like a fortress or a prison in an effort to sabotage your self-worth and self-image. Or perhaps he tries to create a looming tower, a castle stretching up along the path of your mind in an effort to distract you from the Spirit's leading. An unholy edifice that keeps you focused on "living in the now" according to the flesh, rather than walking with your eyes shut tight, leaning upon the Spirit every step of the way. These are strongholds. They are not instantly torn down, but it is a process of the renewing work of the present-day deliverance ministry of Jesus Christ operating in your life.

The enemy tries to trap us behind mental and emotional bars, so that we view life through the *illusion of bondage* in our minds. Strongholds are mental and emotional assaults against us, which can only be completely overcome by working with the Spirit's power. There are basically two types of strongholds: rational ones, and irrational ones. (Dr. Carole Jenne)

Rational strongholds relate to the logical thought process of the mind. I'm not saying that "thinking" is a stronghold; I mean when one uses his or her own flawed reasoning that is unilluminated by the Spirit to "puzzle out" the problems they face, this can lead to a wrong notion that this fallen, fleshly realm is somehow superior to the heavenly realm of God's secret place. "I cannot change, because this is just the way things are." One might say, I was born with an addictive personality, and this is why I am an alcoholic. This kind of thinking creates a "mind-blinder" that inhibits the earthbound spirit from reaching out to *the* Spirit.

"Casting down imaginations, and every high thing that exalteth itself against the knowledge of God, and bringing into captivity every thought to the obedience of Christ..." (2 Corinthians 10:5 KJV)

The NKJ renders "imaginations" as "arguments," and it is more appropriate to a modern reader, since *imagination* conjures up fanciful creativity to us. Children imagining they're astronauts or princesses. However, the Greek word is *logismos* ("lah-geese-moss," Strong's #3053) and means "a reckoning, computation, reasoning that is hostile to the Christian faith, a judgment or conscious decision." To reckon, count, compute, to reason and consider. You will undoubtedly recognize "logic" stemming from the word.

"Because that, when they knew God, they glorified him not as God, neither were thankful; but became vain in their imaginations, and their foolish heart was darkened." (Romans 1:21 KJV)

Again the New King James renders it "futile in their thoughts," and this is the Greek word *dialogismos* ("dee-ah-lah-geese-moss," Strong's #1261), which is to deliberate with oneself, "inward reasoning, questioning what is true, hesitating, doubting, disputing, arguing." Internalized, it's a discussion with yourself, musing and ruminating; externalized, it is a debate with another. You'll see the English word "dialogue" coming from here.

These "imaginations" can develop into strongholds of natural reasoning that start to dictate all kinds of lies in the mind. The enemy uses these to control and dominate your obedience and faith in God. Quite literally, the enemy begins to control your thoughtlife, and your thoughts will in turn control you!

Irrational strongholds are fears and worries about things that might not even happen. A mind control based on potentialities that might not ever occur. "What if I contract a terminal disease and die early?" Or, "What if I become an addict like my mother?"

The only way to tear down and demolish rational and irrational strongholds is by the aggressive power of the Holy Spirit operating in your mind and emotions as you yield your will to Him. The battle is fought spiritually, but it takes place in the "plains" of your mind. Making war in this way is a type of deliverance, and it is vital in our walk to the Snake Line. Thankfully, the weapons the Lord has placed at our disposal are more than adequate to overcome any enemy, for He has given us the power to bind and to loose.

The Power to Bind and Loose

In Matthew 16, Peter confesses Jesus to be the Christ (Anointed One) of God as well as His Son. The Lord tells Peter only the Father could have revealed this. I have discussed this passage in many other writings, but it is worth revisiting the understanding that "binding and loosing"—the keys of the kingdom that Jesus speaks of in Verse 19—is rooted in the revelation of this Rock that Jesus built His church upon. It's as if Jesus told Peter, "You have revealed My anointing, and these are the keys to release that anointing on this earth..."

The revelation of this statement, "You are the Christ, the Son of the living God" (Matthew 16:16), is threefold. We know that Christ means the "Anointed One," and a son or daughter is one who is—prayerfully!—disciplined by their parents, chastened and molded as they grow into moraled and righteous people. The "Disciplined One." As they mature, it is to be hoped that a grown son or daughter now has the foundation and tools to discipline themselves.

Since we are the children of God, our heavenly Father corrects us as earthly parents do their own children. (Proverbs 3:12; Hebrews 12:6) The living God, our Father, is the "Creative One," who fashions all life, just by the words that proceed from His mouth.

Thus, "the *anointing* comes upon us so that we might *discipline ourselves* to *speak creatively* into any situation and set the captives free." (Dr. Chuck Flynn) In this position, anointed and disciplined under Christ's rule, we are able to stand against any stronghold and see the creative power of His kingdom released—loosed—to bind (or break down) whatever blocks our path to the Snake Line.

It's as if Jesus was saying, "Whatever you prohibit down here on earth, I'll back you up and prohibit it in heaven." That means whatever is *already* prohibited in heaven. Conversely, "Whatever you permit on this earth, I'll open up the heavens and send it down to you." That means whatever is *already* loosed up in heaven.

But I also want you to keep in mind the flipside of these statements—there is also a *negative* connotation to binding and loosing that we often overlook. What I mean by this is, whatever we *permit* (loose) here on earth in the name of fleshly, worldly activity, the Lord will also permit the enemy to feed upon. If we allow an open door, Jesus will not close it for us. Conversely, whatever we forbid (bind) here on earth, in the name of the Spirit's freedom to operate in our lives, Jesus will not force us to allow.

Oftentimes, people are trying to bind demons when they are bound themselves. It doesn't work.

The concepts of binding and loosing are rooted in our freewill. God gives *us* the ability to allow or disallow our activity—for good or for ill. And while it is a strong statement, there is probably an element of truth, regarding death before one's time, to permitting something to continue that one should not, or not permitting something to happen that should. That's certainly not a judgmental statement; we all have to grow in our understanding of these truths concerning binding and loosing, but we must make sure that we are not a hindrance to the ministry of Jesus Christ in our lives by doing something we know we shouldn't be doing, or *not* doing something we know we *should* be doing.

Keep this also in the front of your thinking as you meditate upon this: I want to reiterate strongly that we are talking about a habitual lifestyle of permitting sin, or forbidding the activity of the Spirit, here.

Many people believe that if they "slip up" once or twice, well, now they have a demon. That is not necessarily the case. No one but God knows at what time indiscretion can open the door to a demonic vexation, so don't take this as license to do "whatever" and think it doesn't matter. But also, if we confess our sins (quickly and earnestly), repent of them, and endeavor to follow wholeheartedly after Jesus, He is faithful to forgive them and cleanse us of our unrighteousness. (1 John 1:9) Praise God!

Repeated sin makes one hardened toward God, callous toward His Spirit, and it is possible that, over time, one's conscience can be seared, being no longer able to distinguish what is right and what is wrong. Or rather, one just doesn't care, at least in a particular area of sin. This is when the enemy has a trespass right to bring oppression.

Make it a habit to remain soft toward God and defiant toward sin. If you stumble, repent quickly and honestly. You can save yourself a lot of future "deliverance needs" by doing so.

Nevertheless, if we have consistently manifested fleshly

activity over a period of time, and the enemy *does* bring vexation, we still have recourse to turn from such and proceed forward on our course to the Lord's mountain.

Because of Christ's *already* won victory over Satan, we have the authority to tear down any strongholds he might be using to gain an advantage over us. And after the binding, we need to do the loosing. It's important we exercise the authority Christ has delegated to us.

There are several principles rooted in this revelation of binding and loosing. The first of these is *proclamation*. When Jesus asked His disciples, "But who do you say that I am?" (Matthew 16:15), He was outlining the importance of proclaiming our understanding of His authority as the Christ of God, the only begotten of the Father. The Gospel and the testimony of Jesus Christ is permitted to execute its inherent authority in Him when we speak it aloud.

Following the proclamation, we need to incorporate *praise* into our speaking. "Let the high praises of God be in their mouth, and a two-edged sword in their hand..." (Psalm 149:6) It is in our praises that the power to bind and loose is found.

Just as we need to make sure we do not *rob* God of His due praises, we need to recognize there is a *promise* of blessing rooted in tithing according to Malachi 3:8-12.

Further, Isaiah 10 speaks of those "who write misfortune" (Verse 1) *robbing* the needy, the widows, the fatherless. The chapter goes on to outline the haughtiness of Assyria, and the Lord declares He has "*robbed* their treasuries." (Verse 13)

There is a principle of *purity* necessary to execute the authority of binding and loosing. Humility is important, recognizing we need to correct unrighteous behavior before seeking to be delivered. It's not effective to bind demons when you're bound yourself. For more on the importance of purity and humility, please refer to *The Panoramic Seer.*

Prayer is another important component to binding and loosing, specifically the prayer of agreement.

"Assuredly, I say to you, whatever you bind on earth will be bound in heaven, and whatever you loose on earth will be loosed in heaven. Again I say to you that if two of you agree on earth concerning anything that they ask, it will be done for them by My Father in heaven. For where two or three are gathered together in My name, I am there in the midst of them." (Matthew 18:18-20)

Verse 20 shows a *personal* importance of bearing our burdens intertwined with other people. We need each other! You know, if you stand before God asking for deliverance, I want you to have something to show for it. People who care about us will lend their support to seeing what needs to be bound, bound, and what needs to be loosed, loosed.

With all of the above, we cannot overlook the importance of the *presence* of God—the Lord promises us He is there in the midst of His people when they gather in His name. We need to make sure we are seeking His manifest presence when we are seeking deliverance.

Often when a spirit needs to be bound, there is an appropriate spirit that needs to be loosed in its place. I want to credit Dr.

Carole Jenne of Rapha Ministries in Erie, Michigan, for compiling the following "list," as it were, in her booklet on strongholds of the mind, and specifically the spirits that need to be bound and loosed in order to see them torn down. I have included this material here with her permission, along with some of my own thoughts.

First John 4 declares that the spirit of antichrist is already operating in the world. John defines "antichrist" as anything that does not confess Jesus Christ has come in the flesh and is of God. (1 John 2:18,22) Antichrist means anti-anointing, and anything that denies Him or rejects His lordship is of an antichrist spirit.

One facet of the present-day deliverance ministry of Jesus Christ is to bind the spirit of antichrist in someone's life and subsequently loose His Spirit in its place.

"But you are not in the flesh but in the Spirit, if indeed the Spirit of God dwells in you. Now if anyone does not have the Spirit of Christ, he is not His." (Romans 8:9)

Being in servitude to anyone or anything on this earth is a stronghold, represented by a spirit of bondage. This speaks of all manner of addiction, not just physical, but mental and emotional as well; relationships, racial strife, even an addiction to religion. All of it must be subjected to the Lord. Thankfully, binding the spirit of bondage makes way to loose the spirit of adoption.

"For you did not receive the spirit of bondage again to fear, but you received the Spirit of adoption by whom we cry out, 'Abba, Father.'" (Romans 8:15)

We are slaves to no one—but rather sons and daughters of

God; indeed, heirs with Christ! We must exercise our wills, working alongside the power of the Spirit, to stand against all the works of the enemy.

Further, we must resist the influence and operation of a spirit of deception. (See the first part of 1 Timothy 4.) Those with the inability to receive the truth of God's Word, or those struggling with the "doctrines" of the world, often need deliverance from a spirit of error or delusion.

But thankfully, "We are of God. He who knows God hears us; he who is not of God does not hear us. By this we know the spirit of truth and the spirit of error." (1 John 4:6)

It is the Spirit of truth that needs to be loosed. "...The Spirit of truth, whom the world cannot receive, because it neither sees Him nor knows Him; but you know Him, for He dwells with you and will be in you." (John 14:17)

There is a spirit of fear according to 2 Timothy 1:7. This speaks of all manner of phobias, personality disorders, passive/aggressive behavior and the like. But God has given us the Spirit of power, love and a sound mind. We need to pursue our path that takes us into the stronghold of the Lord, instead of the strongholds of the mind.

Pride is a spirit that must be bound. "Pride goes before destruction, and a haughty spirit before a fall. Better to be of a humble spirit with the lowly, than to divide the spoil with the proud." (Proverbs 16:18-19) Any kind of self-importance, especially mixed with a lack of esteem for others, is a stronghold. Those who are ultra-aggressive, domineering, critical of others—these need a Spirit of humility loosed. The fruit of the Spirit is recognized by gentleness and self control. (Galatians 5:23)

"Therefore lay aside all filthiness and overflow of wickedness, and receive with meekness the implanted word, which is able to save your souls." (James 1:21)

"God resists the proud, but gives grace to the humble." (Proverbs 3:34)

"Humble yourselves in the sight of the Lord, and He will lift you up." (James 4:10)

"For thus says the High and Lofty One who inhabits eternity, whose name is Holy: 'I dwell in the high and holy place, with him who has a contrite and humble spirit, to revive the spirit of the humble, and to revive the heart of the contrite ones.'" (Isaiah 57:15)

The first part of Isaiah 61 speaks of the Lord comforting "all who mourn" by giving them a "garment of praise for the spirit of heaviness." Many people—Christians included—lack the peace to act wisely in their daily decisions. A sense of futility and bleakness permeates their thoughtlife—a consuming feeling of malaise and despair cripples them by keeping them in a state of dejection and defeatism. This is a stronghold in the lives of many well-meaning people, but thankfully the power of the Spirit is present to His children to imbue within them a feeling of hope, which brings joy and peace.

"Now may the God of hope fill you with all joy and peace in believing, that you may abound in hope by the power of the Holy Spirit." (Romans 15:13)

"Why are you cast down, O my soul? And why are you disquieted within me? Hope in God; for I shall yet praise Him, the help of my countenance and my God." (Psalm 43:5)

Some may need to bind the spirit of jealousy and loose a spirit of love. Jealousy is an overpowering desire to make something (or someone) your own. God says His name is Jealous in Exodus 34:14. "Or do you think that the Scripture says in vain, 'The Spirit who dwells in us yearns jealously'?" (James 4:5)

But when we speak of a stronghold of jealousy we are outlining the negative, or perverted, aspects of a "proper jealousy," so to speak, that we are to have for the Lord. This negative kind of jealousy stems from suspicious thoughts, a sense of rivalry and antagonism, bitter feelings of umbrage and resentment. It manifests as strife, violent outbursts, slandering.

Pretty much the opposite of love—which is what the Lord's jealousy is rooted in. By releasing a spirit of love, we become firmly rooted in having "jealous" thoughts only of the Lord— nothing else this earth can offer us compares to Him. We desire no one else except Him.

"Whom have I in heaven but You? And there is none upon earth that I desire besides You." (Psalm 73:25)

Isaiah 19:14 tells us the Lord mixed a "perverse spirit" in the midst of the Egyptians, so that everything they set out to do was performed as a vomiting, staggering drunk man. That's a pretty harsh visual!

Perverseness in its simplest expression is contrary behavior, obstinacy, stubbornness, to be opposite in one's nature—it implies an act of the will, a byproduct of rebellion, and manifests as aberrant behavior, such as in the case of homosexuality.

The power of the Spirit is such that we might obey the Truth as revealed in God's Word. "Since you have purified your souls in obeying the truth through the Spirit in sincere love of the brethren, love one another fervently with a pure heart... submitting to one another in the fear of God." (1 Peter 1:22; Ephesians 5:21)

Laziness can be a stronghold, rooted in the spirit of stupor or sloth, what Isaiah 29:9-11 calls a blinding "spirit of deep sleep." This type of mindset leads to listless inactivity, an indifference toward things of the Spirit, a slowness to react to what He is wanting to do in one's life, making one lethargically apathetic and unconcerned about their place in the Lord.

I have maintained through the course of several books that the miracles of God are given to shake people out of this lukewarm limpness, releasing a spirit of zeal in its wake. This is why I am always alarmed when Christians downplay the present-day ministry of Jesus Christ in the name of signs and wonders. As if we have somehow "outgrown" the need for them! And it has produced entire generations of bored, underwhelmed disciples.

Fervency and ardor are the byproducts of the release of the miraculous. It is His manifested power in our daily lives that keeps us burning "white hot" for Him and "not lagging in diligence, fervent in spirit, serving the Lord..." (Romans 12:11)

"...As His divine power has given to us all things that pertain to life and godliness, through the knowledge of Him who called us by glory and virtue, by which have been given to us exceedingly great and precious promises, that through these you may be partakers of the divine nature, having escaped the corruption that is in the world through lust. But also for this very reason, giving all diligence, add to your faith virtue, to virtue knowledge, to knowledge self-control, to self-control perseverance, to perseverance godliness, to godliness brotherly kindness, and to brotherly kindness love. For if these things are yours and abound, you will be neither barren nor unfruitful in the knowledge of our Lord Jesus Christ." (2 Peter 1:3-8)

This is a "must-have" list that Peter outlines. But how exactly are we to "add to" our faith all these things without the due "all diligence" part? And how are we to maintain a spirit of zeal if we are spiritually indolent? This takes the power of Jesus operating in our lives to shatter a spirit of lassitude.

It sort of ties in to this last type of stronghold I want to address, which is a spirit of whoredom. It's a strong word that conjures up all types of ill-reputed concepts, but here I mean it specifically as the Lord perceives idolatry—a type of harlotry, prostituting ourselves out to other lovers. God never minced words concerning this, and I don't think we should either. Let's call it what He calls it: spiritual whoremongering.

"My people ask counsel from their wooden idols, and their staff informs them. For the spirit of harlotry has caused them to stray, and they have played the harlot against their God... They do not direct their deeds toward turning to their God, for the spirit of harlotry is in their midst, and they do not know the Lord." (Hosea 4:12; 5:4)

Occult practices, sorcery, necromancy, paganism, witchery, black magic, white magic, spellcasting and incantations all fall under this category. But also, anything else that makes God second place in your life is idolatry. You may think, I don't consort with palm readers and psychics! But the Bible states that any "friendship" with the world system is a form of spiritual adultery.

"Adulterers and adulteresses! Do you not know that friendship with the world is enmity with God? Whoever therefore wants to be a friend of the world makes himself an enemy of God." (James 4:4)

In and of ourselves, even with the purest of intentions, we cannot stay faithful to God apart from His love flowing through us. We are merely the reciprocators of His love. "We love Him because He first loved us." (1 John 4:19) This means even when we were "playing the harlot" He never stopped loving us. What an amazing Bridegroom we have!

It takes His Spirit having free reign in our lives to tear down these strongholds. We need to allow Him to loose a spirit of "judgment and burning" in our midst.

"When the Lord has washed away the filth of the daughters of Zion, and purged the blood of Jerusalem from her midst, by the spirit of judgment and by the spirit of burning..." (Isaiah 4:4)

"But who can endure the day of His coming? And who can stand when He appears? For He is like a refiner's fire and like launderers' soap. He will sit as a refiner and a purifier of silver; He will purify the sons of Levi, and purge them as gold and silver, that they may offer to the Lord an offering in righteousness." (Malachi 2:2-3)

"John answered, saying to all, 'I indeed baptize you with water; but One mightier than I is coming, whose sandal strap I am not worthy to loose. He will baptize you with the Holy Spirit and fire.'" (Luke 3:16)

This is our Bridegroom, our King! This is the present-day deliverance ministry of Jesus Christ! He is a mighty warrior and He is preparing His Bride for war.

"For the weapons of our warfare are not carnal but mighty in God for pulling down strongholds..."

—2 Corinthians 10:4

5

Preparing for War

The Greek for "weapons" in 2 Corinthians 10:4 implies a tool or instrument for preparing something (Strong's #3696), in this case making war. It is translated "armor" twice (see Romans 13:12; 2 Corinthians 6:7.)

"Warfare" is the Greek word *strateia* ("strah-tie-uh," Strong's #4752), which you'll recognize in English as *strategy*. It is also the same word Paul uses again when charging Timothy to war "a good warfare" with the prophetic words given to him (1 Timothy 1:18), again implying a need for prophetic revelation when combating the onslaught of the enemy. *Strateia* defines a military campaign or expedition and comes from the root for a soldier on active duty being led by a commander into battle—being posted to a particular duty after being sent out from the encampment. That is, the directions and orders a soldier is given to complete his or her mission. Spiritually speaking, all of this implies being led by the Holy Spirit and following His directions to the letter.

So we could paraphrase, "the tools of our strategy are not carnal..." That is *sarkikos* in the Greek ("sar-key-koss," Strong's #4559), meaning "pertaining to flesh." The word speaks of being under the control of animal appetites, aroused by the animal nature, as opposed to being governed by God. The root of the word is most strictly "meat," that is the flesh of a body stripped (literally "swept clean" or "brushed off") of skin, which covers the bones and is permeated by blood.

It does not always imply the depravity of human nature (though that is certainly part of the definition), but also includes mental exercises, reasoning faculties, and human effort—that is, our natural talent, which is not always a bad thing. God gave you a brain and physical strength so you could use them!

However, when dealing with strongholds, mere human flesh is not capable of tearing them down. It takes "mighty" (powerful) weapons and strategies belonging to the capacity of God alone to "pull down" these raised fortresses. That is an interesting phrase in the Greek as well: *kathairesis* ("kuh-thigh-rih-sis," Strong's #2506.)

You might recognize "catharsis" which has a similar preposition, but which in the Greek means "to make clean, to cleanse, to purge (the body)." *Kathairesis*, on the other hand, implies a demolition; it is translated "destruction" elsewhere in the New Testament and can figuratively mean "extinction."

The city of Jericho was "pulled down" by spiritual weapons (Joshua 5-6), and I think it provides a great analogy for us, preparing to "take the land" as it were. Our "Joshua"—that is, Jesus—destroyed the power of the enemy spiritually so that we might possess our inheritance. Notice the two primary weapons that brought about the fall of Jericho: shouting and marching. Shouting released the power of God through their mouths. Marching speaks of a militant, ordered, unwavering, unflagging walk in obedience—just as ours is to be as we walk the path to the Lord's mountain.

"See, I have set the land before you; go in and possess the land which the Lord swore to your fathers—to Abraham, Isaac, and Jacob—to give to them and their descendants after them." (Deuteronomy 1:8)

Pulling down strongholds is the destruction of fortresses, either raised up within ourselves, or raised up without—in the world at large. The principles here are valid for both, but I want to point out that you cannot reign outwardly until you have reigned inwardly. Oftentimes, out of zeal, well-meaning Christians attempt to bring down strongholds out there in the world before they have conquered their own lands, and it's a similar concept to leaving the "back door" open for the enemy to sneak right in. My point is, possess your personal land before taking more. Books like this can help you with that, by outlining these spiritual weapons of war.

Why would God give us weapons if there wasn't a fight? We know that Satan's power is shattered by the conquering Lord, and yet we still must press our rights, so to speak, and maintain the victory that has already been won. What we war against is the enemy's onslaught against our confidence in God's power and His Word.

The promise given to Joshua applies to us spiritually today. "Every place that the sole of your foot will tread upon I have given you, as I said to Moses. " (Joshua 1:3)

Okay, so what kinds of weapons are we talking about here?

First is the mighty, matchless name of Jesus. (Again, see

Philippians 2:9-11.) "And they overcame him by the blood of the Lamb and by the word of their testimony, and they did not love their lives to the death." (Revelation 12:11)

Exodus 17:15 reveals a covenant name of the Lord: Yahweh-Nissi, "the Lord is my Banner." Just as a standard is raised on the battlefield to unite the troops, the name of Jesus is a rallying point to execute the authority that is behind the name. It is by this name we have the right to trample down the enemy before us as an overwhelming onslaught. When you use the name of Jesus, use it as if He were standing there beside you—a Banner raised on the battlefield.

But I also want to point out that the authority and power behind the name of Jesus isn't automatically inherent. Just shouting the name at the enemy, without the knowledge and understanding of who is standing behind the name, won't do any good. "You believe that there is one God. You do well. Even the demons believe—and tremble!" (James 2:19)

The authority in the name of Jesus is something that must be laid hold of through the exercise of our spirits as we grow in a personal relationship with Him. The name is activated by the power of the Spirit in response to our faith. It is not a magic password, but rather a deep comprehension of the Person to whom the name represents.

"Because he has set his love upon Me, therefore I will deliver him; I will set him on high, because he has known My name. He shall call upon Me, and I will answer him; I will be with him in trouble; I will deliver him and honor him." (Psalm 91:14-15)

That phrase "he has set his love upon Me" is quite unique in the Hebrew. It's the word *chashaq* (kha-shack, Strong's #2836), meaning "to be attached to, to long for, to cleave or cling to, to have a delight or desire in, to adhere to, to be joined to." It is also interchangeable with another Hebrew word meaning "to withhold, to keep back, refrain, keep in check, to preserve, assuage, to spare, to keep back for oneself." (See Strong's #2820.) Most interestingly, *chashaq* can mean "to band together, to cover over, to fillet," as in Exodus 27 where the pillars of the court were overlaid, banded, or filleted with silver.

Therefore, "setting our love" on the Lord means we have attached ourselves to Him, longing for Him only, delighting in our desire for Him; and because of this, He keeps us back for Himself, preserving us, reining us in, so that we might be covered over, filleted by His power and love. What an awesome concept!

Next, is His Word. The name of Jesus is built upon our standing foundation of what is written in the Bible, which is built upon the "good ground" of our heart. (Mark 4:1-20) If we are built upon the Rock, rather than the sand, Satan cannot move us. (Matthew 7:24-27)

"All Scripture is given by inspiration of God, and is profitable for doctrine, for reproof, for correction, for instruction in righteousness, that the man of God may be complete, thoroughly equipped for every good work." (2 Timothy 3:16-17)

Paul earlier had told Timothy, "If you instruct the brethren in these things, you will be a good minister of Jesus Christ, nourished in the words of faith and of the good doctrine which you have carefully followed." (1 Timothy 4:6)

A good minister—and an overcoming saint—is well-nourished by the words of faith and good doctrine that are carefully followed. We must love His Word, "...For You have magnified Your word above all Your name." (Psalm 138:2)

Faith is a powerful weapon in our hand. It is His faith in Himself working with our faith in Him that is our release from the strongholds that imprison us. Faith is what gives us the ability to renounce the enemy and then proclaim the name of Jesus based upon what we have learned in His Word. This application of faith should always be spoken and released. Speak it out against the devil.

"Resist him, steadfast in the faith, knowing that the same sufferings are experienced by your brotherhood in the world. But may the God of all grace, who called us to His eternal glory by Christ Jesus, after you have suffered a while, perfect, establish, strengthen, and settle you." (1 Peter 5:9-10)

"Resist" recalls the notion I mentioned earlier, to "show forth your discipline," and that's what Peter is referring to in Verse 6: "Therefore humble yourselves under the mighty hand of God, that He may exalt you in due time."

In the Greek, the word resist is *anthistemi* ("on-this-tay-me," Strong's #436) and is comprised of the prefix "anti" and the root *histemi*, meaning "standing firm or still." Literally, "to stand against," it implies properly standing on one's feet, compared to *tithemi* ("tee-thay-me," Strong's #5087) which means to lay down or kneel.

The word steadfast is *stereos* (seriously! Only it's pronounced "steh-reh-oss," Strong's #4731), meaning "strong, firm, stable, solid, immovable, hard, rigid, stiff, sure, stubborn." It, too, comes from the root *histemi*. (Strong's #2476)

So "resist steadfast" means "stand on your feet stubbornly in one place, strongly, firmly, rigidly against" the devil in faith. As we do so, the grace of God will perfect, establish, strengthen and settle us.

Perfect is *katartizo* ("kah-tar-tee-zoh," Strong's #2675), meaning "to render thoroughly complete, to fit or frame, to mend soundly, to arrange and adjust until perfected."

Establish is *sterizo* ("stay-ree-zoh," Strong's #4741), and it comes from the roots of *histemi* and *stereos*. It means "to make stable, to set firmly, to fix, to render constant," literally, "to turn resolutely in a certain direction."

Strengthen is *sthenoo* ("sthey-nah-oh," Strong's #4599) and also comes from *histemi*. (See a pattern here?) This word speaks of bodily vigor, "to make strong."

Lastly, settle is *themelioo* ("the-mell-ee-ah-oh," Strong's #2311), which means "to lay a basis for." This means "to lay a stable foundation, to erect or to found, to be grounded," and comes from the root mentioned above, *tithemi*—"to lay down."

All of these attributes are worked out by the grace of God based on our resisting the devil steadfastly in the faith. Our faith is the victory that has overcome the world. (1 John 5:4)

"Fight the good fight of faith, lay hold on eternal life, to which you were also called and have confessed the good confession in the presence of many witnesses." (1 Timothy 6:12)

Colossians 1:13 tells us we have been delivered from darkness and conveyed into Christ's kingdom. The means by which this has happened is based solely on our New Testament covenant position, which is ratified by the blood of Jesus. His blood is the means by which we are rightly related to God and is, thus, an extremely powerful weapon. Our covenant with the Lord breaks all other previous pacts we have made with the enemy and his world system. We have been redeemed, bought out of slavery to a corrupt taskmaster, and made joint heirs with Christ. (Romans 8:17) No one can make a verbal accusation stand against us because of the blood of Jesus.

Before we leave this section, I would like to share one more extremely powerful Weapon that God has given us, which is the Key to unlocking all the others: that is, of course, His Spirit.

First Corinthians 6:17 tells us, "But he who is joined to the Lord is one spirit with Him." This joining is a process of growing in relationship with the Spirit. What's great about this process is that the more you grow in it, the less power you always need. What I mean by that is, as we deepen our relationship with Him, the Spirit expands so much in our lives that He outshines, outweighs, any attack from the enemy. This is truly living under the shadow of the Almighty, living above the Snake Line. It should be the ultimate goal of the believer to develop such a relationship with the Holy Spirit that, "...He would grant you, according to the riches of His glory, to be strengthened with might through His Spirit in the inner man..." (Ephesians 3:16)

The prayer of command, the rebuking, the binding and loosing, even the high praise of shouting and marching, are incapable of being separated from our level of connection to God's Spirit, based on the blood of Jesus, the power of His name as revealed in His Word, and our faith in Him.

Principalities, Powers, Rulers, and Hosts

On the other side of the battlefield, I want to take a few moments to outline the types of demonic activity the enemy employs in order to erect strongholds of the mind. Now, I know this is a book on the present-day deliverance ministry of Jesus Christ; but as I have said in other writings, I am not going to debate whether or not a Christian can have a demon. After forty-some years of full-time ministry, I am pretty well set in my convictions concerning this, and it is pointless to discuss the semantics of demonic oppression in a Christian's walk. Let it suffice to say if a Christian cannot be "possessed" by a demon, he or she most certainly can be influenced or suppressed or oppressed by one— not in their inward spirit-man, for that is the residing place of the Holy Spirit; but in the soulish realm or in the body, at the very least, the demonic can hamper a Christian's lifestyle. In any case, deliverance is needed. Fair enough? Let's move on.

"Finally, my brethren, be strong in the Lord and in the power of His might. Put on the whole armor of God, that you may be able to stand against the wiles of the devil. For we do not wrestle against flesh and blood, but against principalities, against powers, against the rulers of the darkness of this age, against spiritual hosts of wickedness in the heavenly places. Therefore take up the whole armor of God, that you may be able to withstand in the evil day, and having done all, to stand." (Ephesians 6:10-13)

This whole passage is in the context of putting on the full armor of God, and it relates specifically to "brethren"—those who are in Christ. Paul is wanting to educate the Ephesian church on the wiles (tricks) of the devil. He outlines a sort of rank and file for the spiritual entities that we "wrestle" against.

This word *pale* ("pah-lay," Strong's #3823) is only used one time in the New Testament, and it means most succinctly "wrestle." *smile* "A contest between two in which each endeavors to throw the other, and which is decided when the victor is able to hold his opponent down with his hand upon his neck." The root of this word means "to vibrate," and in another form means "to cast, throw or scatter something without caring where it falls," even referring to dung.

"Principalities" is *arche* ("ar-hay," where the "H" sounds like one is clearing the throat; Strong's #746), and this word signifies an individual who holds the highest, loftiest position in rank and authority. It is speaking of the "origin or beginning of something," the first in a series, and therefore, the leader. It means the "extremity of something (like the corners of a sail)," and it refers to the "first place of rule (magistracy.)" These are the highest and strongest of the demonic host. This would be like the "Prince of Persia" in Daniel 10. It is my opinion, and I believe I am right, that we do not confront these levels of spirits on our own. These are beings that the warring angels deal with.

(As an aside of caution, we must be absolutely sure we are being guided and led by the Spirit when "waging war" in the name of spiritual mapping or intense intercession when dealing with principalities. I find very little, if any, scriptural evidence for this kind of engagement on our part. Note it was the special miracles God wrought through Paul that tackled the spirits controlling Ephesus—not him confronting them personally. See Acts 19:11. Thus ends the sermon.)

"Powers" is *exousia* ("ex-ooh-see-uh," Strong's #1849.) This is the "ability to do something." "The power of choice to do as one pleases, leave or permission, authority, influence, rights and privileges." It is a sense of ability and is translated "jurisdiction" in Luke 23:7. The word speaks of delegated authority—so the principalities giving power, or authority, to the next level of spiritual entities. I believe this is the level of the demonic that we confront.

"Rulers" comes from *kosmokrator* ("kah-smah-krah-toar," Strong's #2888) which is only used in the New Testament referring to the devil and his demons, the "princes of the age," or the "lords of the world" (system.) In rabbinic writings, it can refer to the death angel. It's a compound word stemming from *kosmos* (where we get "cosmos") and *kratos* which means "power or dominion." This is speaking of raw, wicked power that has been arranged into some kind of order. Think of it kind of like a military training camp where recruits with raw power are taught discipline and how to focus that power together as soldiers in an army. It isn't willy-nilly, each spirit out for itself, but rather a coordinated effort organized by the higher ranking demons, sent out to commit violence and destruction throughout the world.

Notice, though, they are only the rulers of the "darkness of this world," (KJV) which can be rendered "the shadows of this age"—the Greek word is where we get "eon." The earth and all it contains belong to the Lord according to Psalm 24:1, but the darkness of this epoch in time belongs to Satan and his minions.

"Spiritual wickedness in high places" (KJV) means malicious and depraved plots and purposes—the schemes of our spiritual enemy—that originate from the beings "above the sky;" that is, the celestial heavens. To make it clear this is referring to the rulers of this age, the NKJ adds "hosts" to the verse.

"...And I saw a star fallen from heaven to the earth. To him was given the key to the bottomless pit." (Revelation 9:1)

David's Key

While all of the above sounds like a real terrible mess we have to deal with, I want to reiterate that each of these levels of demonic spirits has been crippled and paralyzed in their activity concerning the redeemed of the Lord.

Yes, there is a spirit that opposes us, but I believe our primary "enemy" is not Satan as much as it is a *spirit of stupor*. By that I mean, the worldly way of thinking, feeling, believing and acting.

A sluggish, lukewarm, indifferent malaise that tries to steal the zeal of the Lord from His people. It is with this spirit we have to be most watchful so we don't succumb to its wiles. There is so much noise out there in the world—all the horrific, depressing things we hear on a daily basis—that it becomes easier to "tune it out," so to speak, and just set the cruise control at 55 while we coast through life until we meet Jesus again.

"For the Lord has poured out on you the spirit of deep sleep, and has closed your eyes, namely, the prophets; and He has covered your heads, namely, the seers." (Isaiah 29:10)

Notice the spirit of deep sleep is upon the prophetic element of the Lord's body. The deception here is that the spirit of stupor can also be a deeply *religious* spirit—the people are content with their ceremonial acts, but all the while, it produces a unenthusiastic attitude concerning the true things of God. This goes back to my earlier statements on the necessity of being activated in a prophetic spirit—one that counteracts this dullness that is so prevalent in the world, and the Church, today.

I have heard a lot of teaching surrounding the "key of David," and while I think it is, for the most part, wonderful and correct, a lot of it seems to focus just on the praise and worship aspect, since David was the great psalmist. And this is absolutely true, but let us not forget that King David was also a *prophetic* psalmist. He had an intuition—inspired by the Holy Spirit, of course— that was undeniably profound, a true perceptive inner vision that really understood the times he was living in. While this was indeed a gift from God, it is something David cultivated throughout his life.

"The key of the house of David I will lay on his shoulder; so he shall open, and no one shall shut; and he shall shut, and no one shall open." (Isaiah 22:22)

I believe this is speaking of a prophetic unction that sadly is lacking in many church circles, or let me soften that and say, it is often downplayed as being esoteric or superfluous. I am sure I have said it at least a dozen times in my writings: the discernment of spirits is something that is greatly undervalued in the modern church as a general rule. (And of course, I know there are many, many exceptions, but if we were to look at the "Church" as a corporate body of Christ, I think you would have to agree with me in the above statement.)

So what is the answer? How do we confront the spirit of limpness and lethargy?

"Now this is the confidence that we have in Him, that if we ask anything according to His will, He hears us. And if we know that He hears us, whatever we ask, we know that we have the petitions that we have asked of Him." (1 John 5:14-15)

That "if we know" part means there is a requirement on our behalves. Something *we* have to work out in order to have the petitions answered. How many people know a well-meaning, sincere Christian who is *not* receiving what they ask according to His will? The Word is not false, there must be something deeper we're not catching ahold of.

"And do not be conformed to this world, but be transformed by the renewing of your mind, that you may prove what is that good and acceptable and perfect will of God." (Romans 12:2)

This verse is saying don't be conformed to this lackadaisical, worldly spirit—there is a renewing of your mind that must take place in order to prove what is the good, acceptable, perfect (singular) will of God. It's those kinds of people that have whatever they ask of Him.

This is the present-day deliverance ministry of Jesus Christ— not just casting out devils in His name, but being delivered in the realm of our thought processes, our emotional balance, as we submit our will to the work of the prophetic Holy Spirit. These kinds of folks live above the Snake Line.

Look, most of us—myself included—aren't there yet, so don't be condemned. Be driven by the zeal of the Lord, because our current lack doesn't negate the truth:

"For whom He foreknew, He also predestined to be conformed to the image of His Son, that He might be the firstborn among many brethren." (Romans 8:29)

The Bible says, "He has delivered us from the power of darkness and conveyed us into the kingdom of the Son of His love..." (Colossians 1:13)

This is a past-tense thing. We are out of the system of darkness the rulers of this world had us shackled to, and yet, "getting saved" is not a full stop. Rather, it's the beginning of a lifelong walk toward the mount of the Lord on the Highway of Holiness, and along the way we are supposed to be so transformed into the image of His dear Son, that we become unrecognizable as "prey" to the enemy. We become so hidden in His life, that our own doesn't give off the stench that calls the vultures. His own power exudes from our very pores, because we are so yielded and conformed (that means "formed with") to Him, the enemy cannot distinguish who is who: the blood-bought saint, or the One in whom all authority over them resides.

"But we all, with unveiled face, beholding as in a mirror the glory of the Lord, are being transformed into the same image from glory to glory, just as by the Spirit of the Lord." (2 Corinthians 3:18)

What this takes is face-to-face encounters with the Lord, by His Spirit, fashioned in the secret place. I do not mean to sound harsh to any of you dear readers—I preach to myself—but I daresay the vast, vast majority of us do not spend enough time simply waiting upon the Lord. And it's not like we're rebellious and don't want to—we all lead extremely busy lives. We're productive, we take care of our children, we work hard jobs, we cultivate our earthly relationships, and that's all well and good. But if we were to be completely frank with ourselves, a lot of our lives are also filled with the noise of this world. And we're so tuned in to it (or tuned *out* as the case may be) that we're easy pickin's for the enemy.

No matter what is going on in our lives, if we want to reach the Snake Line, things are going to have to be restructured so that we get to a point of living in the secret place, coming down long enough to cook dinner, pay our bills, spend some time with the kiddos, and then we climb back up the mountain.

Now look, I'm not saying neglect your duties. I'm not saying neglect your families. You can take these concepts so far the other way that you're of no use to anyone more earthbound than you. I said it earlier, not all of us can spend six hours a day in high praise and worship and still keep the lights turned on.

I am saying things are out of balance, not that we must live to any one extremity. That's no good either. Keep things in perspective while you read this book, please. Don't forget that the Lord came that you may have and *enjoy life* more abundantly, to the full, till it overflows. (John 10:10 AMP) Take your kids to the park, have a bite of ice cream now and again, walk your dog, go for a swim, listen to music, knit a sweater, watch a football game, whatever... but also, don't neglect the importance of living in the Lord's shadow.

The key to all this is to embrace the Person of Jesus as the Christ ("the Anointed One") in order to be elevated above the mental and emotional harassment, the noise, that surrounds you.

"It shall come to pass in that day that his burden will be taken away from your shoulder, and his yoke from your neck, and the yoke will be destroyed because of the anointing oil." (Isaiah 10:27)

The word "anointing" in the Hebrew is *shemen* ("sheh-men," Strong's #8081), and the root of the word means "to grow fat." So the connotation here is, we become so spiritually fat that the yoke will not go around our necks! What an awesome word picture!

To be changed into Christ's image is to become Christlike *in the anointing*. That is what breaks off the spirit of stupor—or any spirit for that matter. Strongholds are destroyed when we are anointed with the prophetic Spirit, just as David was. That's the key.

How does one become anointed? Only by cultivating one's relationship with Jesus—there is no shortcut. Greater time must be spent ministering to the Lord if we want to see ourselves decrease so that He might increase. (John 3:30) Remember that anointing cannot be poured out on flesh. (Exodus 30:32) It takes a dedicated worshipper of Jesus to live above the Snake Line, and we must all grow in that area if we want to see an end to the enemy's harassment in our lives.

"...That you put off, concerning your former conduct, the old man which grows corrupt according to the deceitful lusts, and be renewed in the spirit of your mind, and that you put on the new man which was created according to God, in true righteousness and holiness."

—Ephesians 4:22-24

6

Our Great Need

eliverance is our great need. It is to be our *passion*, our *possession*, our *prayer*, and our *purpose*. My definition of deliverance is more an all-inclusive word than what most of us think of when we hear "deliverance." It probably conjures up images of some four-hour marathon session ("Come out!" "No, we don't want to!") and foaming at the mouth. While that *can* be what deliverance means, when I use it generally, I mean it as "liberty from the dictates of the flesh and the demons that feed on it." Matthew 24:28 tells us, "For wherever the carcass is, there the eagles will be gathered together."

Deliverance does not need to be scary; it is supposed to be a way of life. After all, deliverance is the children's bread. (Matthew 15:26) Being renewed in the "spirit of your mind" (Ephesians 4:23) means to bring the actions of the body under the Lordship of the Spirit.

We are warned that, "Whoever has no rule over his own spirit is like a city broken down, without walls." (Proverbs 25:28) And, "He who digs a pit will fall into it, and whoever breaks through a wall will be bitten by a serpent." (Ecclesiastes 10:8) But Proverbs 16:32 says, "He who is slow to anger is better than the mighty, and he who rules his spirit than he who takes a city."

It's important, then, to our way of life to have the proper walls raised, protection against an outside enemy that would try to run over us roughshod and rob all that the Lord wants us to inherit. A lifestyle of deliverance, as one aspect of our spiritual inheritance, is vital to keeping the hedges up in our minds, wills and emotions.

"Therefore I run thus: not with uncertainty. Thus I fight: not as one who beats the air." (1 Corinthians 9:26)

Deliverance is not some willy-nilly recitation of prayer with a hope that Jesus drives the nasties away. Rather, it is a well-honed weapon we can be equipped with to wield against the enemy. It is an incredibly important, and sadly often overlooked, element of the present-day ministry of Jesus Christ.

"I say then: Walk in the Spirit, and you shall not fulfill the lust of the flesh. For the flesh lusts against the Spirit, and the Spirit against the flesh; and these are contrary to one another, so that you do not do the things that you wish. But if you are led by the Spirit, you are not under the law." (Galatians 5:16-18) Paul goes on to outline what it means to "walk in the flesh" versus "walking in the Spirit" throughout the remainder of the chapter.

When we downplay the importance of deliverance in our Christian circles, we do an injustice to the Spirit of liberty who wants us free to walk according to Him along the path to the Snake Line. Especially those of us who are ministers to the body of Christ. I believe we have a mandate from the Lord to present *all* that He purchased on Calvary, otherwise we slight the people desperate to find that path. "For they have healed the hurt of the daughter of My people slightly, saying, 'Peace, peace!' when there is no peace." (Jeremiah 8:11)

"Then Jesus went into the temple of God and drove out all those who bought and sold in the temple, and overturned the tables of the money changers and the seats of those who sold doves." (Matthew 21:12)

In this passage, we see the Lord is cleansing the temple and driving out the thieves. This is a picture of deliverance. He was passionate about keeping His Father's place holy, sanctified, swept clean as it were. We need to have the same passion for our own temples.

"Or do you not know that your body is the temple of the Holy Spirit who is in you, whom you have from God, and you are not your own? For you were bought at a price; therefore glorify God in your body and in your spirit, which are God's." (1 Corinthians 6:19-20)

I believe God permitted the thieves to be in the temple so that Jesus might drive them out, thereby revealing His lion nature. (Isaiah 42:13; Psalm 68:1) Since Jesus is incapable of changing His nature (Hebrews 13:8), this tells us that His intentions are the same today: our temples (that is, our bodies, including our minds, wills and emotions) must be kept free and clear of defilement.

Our overall salvation throughout the course of our lives into eternity is a process. We're all aware of this, I'm sure. It starts at the moment of salvation, dealing with our past, where we are removed from the penalty of sin; but in the ongoing present, we are being removed from the power of sin as we are sanctified by yielding to the Lord's work through His Spirit. And of course, in the future, we will be removed from the very presence of sin when we return to our Lord.

But in the interim, we need to place as much emphasis on deliverance as we do the other tools the Lord has given us in His present-day ministry as our High Priest.

Mark 7:27 proves deliverance is the children's bread; that's our possession, our inheritance in the Lord, and Jesus admonishes us to pray to the Father to give us our daily bread. (Matthew 6:11) This is why the Lord's Prayer closes with, "And do not lead us into temptation, but deliver us from the evil one. For Yours is the kingdom and the power and the glory forever. Amen" (Verse 13) I believe this verse is specifically emphasizing our personal temple—the kingdom that resides within us, since we are the temple of the Holy Spirit. Our great High Priest is intent on giving us what we need to keep His temple (us) swept clean.

But, still, it is something that we must take for ourselves—it isn't an automatic occurrence. The Lord has given us the bread, but we still must take it. Many well-meaning Christians have a flawed notion that all deliverance takes place the moment they get saved. While this is true in the spirit man, it isn't the case for the rest of your existence.

"And it shall come to pass that whoever calls on the name of the Lord shall be saved. For in Mount Zion and in Jerusalem there shall be deliverance, as the Lord has said, among the remnant whom the Lord calls." (Joel 2:32)

"Walking in the Spirit" requires steps on our part. We must possess our possession. "But on Mount Zion there shall be deliverance, and there shall be holiness; the house of Jacob shall possess their possessions." (Obadiah 17)

Notice the deliverance comes before the holiness. We cannot have true holiness without the deliverance taking place first. Our land of possession is the land of our mind, will and emotions. Deliverance, to me, means not just casting out demons, as important as that is, but also the inner healing that comes from removing the bruises of Satan: fear, rejection, guilt, grief. Shutting opened doors, tearing down strongholds. First the thieves must be driven out, and then after that the Lord can begin rebuilding what was trampled on by the enemy.

This is the process of moving above the Snake Line. I've written elsewhere about how sin must be cleansed, flesh must be crucified, and demons must be cast out. This is the process of living in Christ's victory. It requires an understanding of the tools, or as Paul puts it, the "armor" Jesus has placed at your disposal.

Body Armor

"Therefore take up the whole armor of God, that you may be able to withstand in the evil day, and having done all, to stand. Stand therefore, having girded your waist with truth, having put on the breastplate of righteousness, and having shod your feet with the preparation of the gospel of peace; above all, taking the shield of faith with which you will be able to quench all the fiery darts of the wicked one. And take the helmet of salvation, and the sword of the Spirit, which is the word of God; praying always with all prayer and supplication in the Spirit, being watchful to this end with all perseverance and supplication for all the saints..." (Ephesians 6:13-18)

The first piece of protection Paul mentions is girding our waist with truth. This is like a spiritual belt of truth cinched around our middle, holding everything up and in, if you don't mind the crude analogy.

Knowing the truth sets one free according to John 8:32—it protects the person's vison and purpose in God. Nearly everyone out in the world, and many in the body of Christ, have a distorted view of Him based on the slanderous lies of the enemy. John 8:44 calls Satan the father of lies. He tries to malign the very character of God to people, because he knows the truth is freeing.

Just as the people of Israel couldn't perceive God correctly in the wilderness, our enemy tries to get us to believe a warped lie that God is just an angry Taskmaster who doesn't care about us in the slightest. That He even enjoys our suffering as if it gives Him some kind of perverted pleasure in torturing humanity. Or if it's not that elaborate, at the very least the devil wants us to think that God has somehow rejected us personally—that He watches out for others, forgives *their* sin, but not ours.

Knowing the Truth, as it is presented in God's Word to humankind, keeps you and me free from self-hatred. "I'm not worth anything," the very root of rejection, which comes from hurts in your life that turn to bitterness. This is slander against yourself, giving you a distorted view of who you are.

Lastly, the devil presents lies that perhaps look good on the surface in an attempt to get people sidetracked from the way they should be walking the path to the secret place. He wants them to accept sugar-coated error as a counterfeit for the truth, so that they follow the path of the lie, instead of the path to God. However, if people knew they were being deceived, they wouldn't be deceived, so it is subtle, this falling into error.

Rather, it makes people dull and complacent instead of alert and ready for action. Paul speaks of "deceiving spirits and doctrines of demons" in 1 Timothy 4:1, and I think we are already seeing the beginnings of this "last day deception" that keeps people drifting along in neutral, listening to the slick, sweet lies of the demonic that are always *close* to the truth, but just not *the* Truth. (John 14:6) The teaching of Universalism is one such lie—the enemy knows it must be subtle; it must sound good on the surface, but underneath, it is misleading deception.

This is why Peter says, "Therefore gird up the loins of your mind, be sober, and rest your hope fully upon the grace that is to be brought to you at the revelation of Jesus Christ..." (1 Peter 1:13)

The apostle is speaking of the belt of truth here. Only the simple, unadulterated truth revealed in God's Word is enough to keep one from falling into deception.

Paul continues with the "breastplate of righteousness." What does a breastplate cover? The vital organs under the ribcage, namely the heart, which speaks to our affections.

Where do we stand as children of God? In the righteousness of Jesus. "For He made Him who knew no sin to be sin for us, that we might become the righteousness of God in Him." (2 Corinthians 5:21)

But the enemy attempts to accuse us that we are not righteous, thereby drawing us away from God—wounding the heart, so that we do not keep our affections solely on Christ, who is our righteousness.

Romans 8:33-34 makes it clear, "Who shall bring a charge against God's elect? It is God who justifies. Who is he who condemns? It is Christ who died, and furthermore is also risen, who is even at the right hand of God, who also makes intercession for us."

"Now salvation, and strength, and the kingdom of our God, and the power of His Christ have come, for the accuser of our brethren, who accused them before our God day and night, has been cast down." (Revelation 12:10)

We cannot accept any condemnation the devil would try to heap upon our heads. No guilt of the past, no failure of the present, because salvation and strength, the power of Christ, the very kingdom of God—which is righteousness, peace and joy according to Romans 14:17—have come. We can permit no confusion concerning this truth.

"There is therefore now no condemnation to those who are

in Christ Jesus, who do not walk according to the flesh, but according to the Spirit." (Romans 8:1)

Not only does the breastplate of righteousness protect us from accusation and condemnation—but also spiritual pride, lest we think more highly of ourselves than we ought. (Romans 12:3)

Romans 3:22 promises the righteousness of God Himself to all and on all who believe *through faith in Jesus Christ.* It is nothing on our part other than faith in Jesus' righteousness that makes us righteous.

Verses 25 and 26 of the same chapter speak of how we are justified by Him. That means to be set aright, to be placed on the path of rightness. We know righteousness means "right-standing" with God—and "justified" can be defined as "just-as-if-I'd" never sinned in the first place.

The gospel of peace is to shod our feet. Feet speak of activity, moving about, getting things done—walking it out. This gospel of peace covers our walk, specifically in sharing the Good News with others.

When Jesus was sharing the Gospel, it stirred up a hornet's nest full of religious leaders; yet notice in Matthew 12, He withdrew when He knew they were plotting to destroy Him, so that it might be fulfilled what Isaiah prophesied: "He will not quarrel nor cry out..." (Verse 19)

Notice Jesus still healed all the great multitudes. (Verse 15) He didn't stop sharing the Gospel, and He answered the Pharisees' loaded questions—He just didn't pick a fight with them. He kept His peace without conceding what He was sharing.

"For I am not ashamed of the gospel of Christ, for it is the power of God to salvation for everyone who believes, for the Jew first and also for the Greek." (Romans 1:16)

The gospel of peace moves our feet in the midst of persecution, and the lies people may spread about us, so that we don't compromise or become passive. The devil would like nothing better than to stifle your movement in spreading the Word by lying to you, "Back off. Don't do so much, and I'll take the pressure off you." He tries to convince us just to give up, sit still, be idle.

But the gospel of peace gives you wisdom on how to share it even in the midst of all the lies floating around you.

Verse 16 says, "...Above all, taking the shield of faith with which you will be able to quench all the fiery darts of the wicked one." What are fiery darts? Doubt, fear and unbelief, or rather disbelief. It was the disbelief of the Israelites that ended up leaving them dead in the wilderness. Disbelief is one of the most damaging sins we can harbor and is therefore one of the prime ways the enemy attacks us. "Has God said...?" It makes the very Word of God unprofitable in our lives.

"For indeed the gospel was preached to us as well as to them; but the word which they heard did not profit them, not being mixed with faith in those who heard it." (Hebrews 4:2)

Unbelief, disbelief, nonbelief, misbelief—these words are similar, and are often used interchangeably, but each can carry a slightly different meaning. I define unbelief as a lack of faith based on inexperience. Someone may not be militantly hard-hearted against the present-day deliverance ministry of Jesus Christ. Only, they've never seen it in action, so it causes unbelief. This is still dangerous, but it is rooted in ignorance more than rebellion.

Disbelief, on the other hand, is an act of refusal, a willful ignorance, so to speak. Seeing something occurring, and yet still not believing it. This is why disbelief is used as a reaction or a response to something shocking. "I can't believe that just happened!" he exclaimed in disbelief.

Nonbelief is simply not having a belief in something, mostly based on unfamiliarity—you don't believe, because you don't know to believe it. Misbelief is believing, but in the wrong thing.

All are dangerous, because ignorance is no excuse, but especially so disbelief. If you know something you should do, something that is good—in this case, faith toward God—and you don't do it, that's sin. (James 4:17; Hebrews 6:1)

It is important that we keep our faith active. We need to get to a place along the path to God's mountain that no matter what we see (or don't see) in the name of Christianity, it will not move us from saying to the enemy, while they shoot darts at us from afar, "It is written..." That settles it for us permanently, simply because it is written in God's Word.

It is when we start to disbelieve that we get into trouble.

"Take the helmet of salvation" implies you have an active responsibility in dealing with these mental strongholds we've been discussing. The mind is the battlefield, and Ephesians 4:23 tells you, "...Be renewed in the spirit of your mind."

The helmet of salvation is the protection our minds have against the vain imaginations, distorted views, and distractions of a shouting enemy. The helmet is what breaks ties to past associations with cults or the occult, mental disorders, irrational thought patterns and the like.

The sword of the Spirit is the Bible. Now, don't be deceived, the devil knows what's in the Bible—perhaps better than most Christians, sad to say. He will attempt to distort and twist the Word to make you question what God is saying through it.

With the Spirit's help, the Bible is not difficult to understand—at least concerning God's will for your life, what you are supposed to do, what you are *not* supposed to do. But the enemy will try to make even the most simple, declarative statements of the Bible seem confusing, or unimportant. "This part, here, it doesn't apply to me and my circumstances."

There is no way to get around not knowing what the Word of God says. All of Jesus' earthly ministry, and indeed, His present-day ministry, is rooted firmly in the Word of God, because He *is* the Word of God. (John 1:1) To the extent you know God's Word is the extent to which your deliverance is manifested.

Lastly, "prayer and supplication in the Spirit" relates to Jude 20-21: "But you, beloved, building yourselves up on your most holy faith, praying in the Holy Spirit, keep yourselves in the love of God, looking for the mercy of our Lord Jesus Christ unto eternal life."

I have heard faith and love called the "power twins." Galatians 5:6 speaks of "faith working through love." "And now abide faith, hope, love, these three; but the greatest of these is love." (1 Corinthians 13:13)

When you boil it down to the most simple terms, all of our problems stem from either a lack of faith or a lack of love. So the point of our spiritual armor is to increase our faith and love toward God. It is faith and love that keep us hidden in Christ above the Snake Line.

"Resist him, steadfast in the faith, knowing that the same sufferings are experienced by your brotherhood in the world. But may the God of all grace, who called us to His eternal glory by Christ Jesus, after you have suffered a while, perfect, establish, strengthen, and settle you."

—1 Peter 5:9-10

7

Know Your Enemy

John 10:10 says our enemy is a thief. Thieves are cunning, quiet, underhanded in their maliciousness. They prowl and sneak, breaking into the homes of the unwary, taking what they want, and tiptoeing out again, with no one the wiser till they waken in the morning to find their home ransacked.

Even though our enemy is crushed and paralyzed, that doesn't make him of entirely no effect if we fall prey to his wiles. It is possible for a blood-bought Christian to be tricked and deceived into thinking everything is secure and all right, when it is not. "...Lest Satan should take advantage of us; for we are not ignorant of his devices." (2 Corinthians 2:11)

The Greek word for "devices" (Strong's #3540) refers to his thoughts, purposes, notions and evil plans for us, his "war schemes" as it were. It also means his general disposition concerning us, what he thinks about us (not very highly, I assure you.) Elsewhere it is translated "mind" or "thoughts," and its root comes from a word meaning "to perceive or understand." In other words, we are told not to be ignorant of how the devil thinks about us—we are to know his mind; how he perceives us, and the schemes, ploys, ruses, conspiracies, he is hatching in order to take advantage of us.

So, we must ask ourselves, then, how does the enemy operate?

What foul "war plan" does he have concerning us? Primarily, he fights against our peace, distracting us in the pressures of life so that we become frustrated and restless, or passive and incoherent. The effect is the same: we take our eyes off the path before us and get sidetracked on bunny trails that lead us nowhere but straight into the lion's open mouth.

If you read Job 1, you'll see a pattern that I believe the devil is bound to concerning Christians. He is permitted to *inspect* for weak links in our armor—in our thoughts, emotions, tongues and bodies—these are the four primary areas he attacks. He is permitted to *influence* through temptation those areas, and if we give in to his tricks, he is permitted to *invade* those areas, bringing defilement wherever his dirty feet tread. When we yield to temptation, we can become deceived.

Just as what happened in Genesis 3 with Eve, he tempts us by sowing seeds of *doubt*, whispering *denial* in our ear concerning God's Word of truth, and ultimately, if he can get us to cooperate with him, bringing us into *disobedience.*

He tries to entice us, or harass us, in an attempt to drive us off the narrow walkway to the Lord's mountain. Once we have taken those steps toward his voice, or if we back "away" from the forward path upward—due to his harassment—we face his defilement. Continuing in one of these two directions, eventually he tries to enslave us, forcing us to continue marching in a way we ought not to go. Ultimately, this brings torment, and we can no longer progressively move toward the shelter of the Almighty.

The enemy operates both from the *outside* and the *inside.* For the first form of attack, we must *resist* him. Not back away in fear and scamper off into the underbrush, but rather stand and set our face as a flint against our adversary. (Isaiah 50:7-8) Again, James 4:7 says he will flee, as long as we don't ignore the first part of that verse: submitting to God.

Jesus makes the distinction between *outside* and *inside*. "'Do you not perceive that whatever enters a man from outside cannot defile him, because it does not enter his heart but his stomach, and is eliminated, thus purifying all foods?' And He said, 'What comes out of a man, that defiles a man. For from within, out of the heart of men, proceed evil thoughts, adulteries, fornications, murders, thefts, covetousness, wickedness, deceit, lewdness, an evil eye, blasphemy, pride, foolishness. All these evil things come from within and defile a man.'" (Mark 7:18-23)

There is a difference between *thoughts of evil*, and *evil thoughts*. (Pay attention here so you don't confuse the two.) Thoughts of evil are whispers from the enemy assailing you from the outside. Even Jesus was tempted by thoughts of evil—externally coming against Him. (Matthew 4) But evil thoughts originate from within. This Jesus never did; He never thought up evil on His own. (Hebrews 4:15)

What comes from within must be *expelled*. This is the traditional concept of deliverance, not only from demonic influence, but from our own corrupted thoughts. In either case, we are to give no place to the devil (again, Ephesians 4:7) for him to merge what comes at us from the outside with what is hidden and crusty on the inside.

Discerning what comes from within requires the Word of God

and the work of the Holy Spirit as we yield to His inspections, rather than the devil's. We would not know of what is decaying on the inside were it not for the illumination of the Spirit using the Word as a surgeon's knife to peel back the junk, so it can be cut out and discarded like so much infected tissue.

"For the word of God is living and powerful, and sharper than any two-edged sword, piercing even to the division of soul and spirit, and of joints and marrow, and is a discerner of the thoughts and intents of the heart." (Hebrews 4:12)

This verse is extremely potent. It declares the Word is living and powerful. Living in the Greek means "having vital power in itself and exerting the same upon the soul, alive, fresh, breathing and efficacious." (Strong's #2198) It is the verb form of *zoe*. Powerful is where we get our English word "energy." It means "active, effectual, operative." (Strong's #1756) The Word has inherent ability to do what Hebrews 4:12 says it does, for it is a living thing.

The Word actually has the ability to divide between what is of the soul (mind, will and emotions) and what is of the spirit-man and what is of the physical body (joints and marrow.) In other words, the Bible has the ability to separate out all three facets of our existence, spirit, soul and body, laying them bare, and discovering what is in our hearts and minds (thoughts and intents.) Nothing can be hidden from the Word of God.

When it speaks of "sharper than any two-edged sword," it means the Word acts like a scalpel—a "single, decisive stroke" rather than hacking something numerous times. (See Strong's

#5114 and #2875.) It's not just exploratory prodding, poking our lives with a stick. This precision slicing "reaches through" (piercing, penetrating, Strong's #1338) every piece of our existence, dividing them asunder (KJV)—that is, cleaving, partitioning, separating our three-fold being into its various pieces. Interestingly, that same Greek word (Strong's #3311) is translated as "gifts" (Hebrews 2:4) in the sense of distributing out something, bestowing, imparting.

It is actually to our benefit that the Bible is able to separate us into our different states of being, for through it, we are able to distinguish what is our soul (*psyche*, "soo-kay," Strong's #5590: the heart and mind of a human; "the seat of the feelings, desires, affections, aversions"); what is our spirit (*pneuma*, "noo-mah," Strong's #4151—the eternal life of a human that comes from the breath of God); and what is our physical body (joints and marrow, Strong's #719; #3452). That word marrow means "that which is closed within"—what is shut up inside the body, as the marrow is enclosed by the bones.

The Greek word for "discerner" (Strong's #2924) is where we get the English word "critic," but not necessarily in the negative connotation it usually has in modern speech. *Constructive* criticism. Being "fit or skilled for judging, decisive, discriminative." The root of the word comes from a Roman procurator who administered justice, an arbiter.

The root for "thoughts" means to ponder, to revolve in the mind, to deliberate. More than just a casual, fleeting thought, the word stems from something that inspirits (actually, "inflames") the mind, what goes around and around in our heads. (See Strong's #1760; #2372; #2380.)

"Intents" comes from a Greek word meaning "reason in the narrower sense, as the capacity for spiritual truth, the higher powers of the soul, the faculty of perceiving divine things, of recognising goodness and of hating evil." (Strong's #1771; #3563)

Lastly, "heart" is truly the word for heart, where we get the English *cardio.* "That organ in the animal body which is the centre of the circulation of the blood, and hence was regarded as the seat of physical life." It also speaks of "the faculty of understanding and intelligence, the will and character" of a being. (Strong's #2588)

This is why Proverbs 4:23 admonishes us, "Keep your heart with all diligence, for out of it spring the issues of life." Heart in the Hebrew is similar to the Greek: "the seat of moral character, the appetites, emotions, passions, courage, the conscience and the determination of will." (Strong's #3820) It is from here that all the "issues of life" spring.

With all of the above, it becomes easy to see how important the separating power of the Word of God becomes for those of us seeking to know ourselves, so that we might rise above the Snake Line.

It is by the Word of God that we come to know exactly what it is we believe. For those of us who *know* what we believe—what has been revealed by the surgical act of the Bible—we can begin to expect to rise above the continual attacks of the enemy because:

"He who believes and is baptized will be saved; but he who

does not believe will be condemned. And these signs will follow those who believe: In My name they will cast out demons; they will speak with new tongues; they will take up serpents; and if they drink anything deadly, it will by no means hurt them; they will lay hands on the sick, and they will recover." (Mark 16:16-18)

One thing I wish to point out in the verses above, the demons are expelled and *then* there is speaking with new tongues. I think they're listed in this order on purpose. We have a lot of Christians out there speaking in tongues who have not yet cast out the demons, you know? The other things in the list, taking up serpents, drinking anything deadly, laying hands on the sick and seeing them recover—these are based on the first two items being taken care of. Just something to consider.

What Are Demons Like?

The phrase "possessed with devils" in the New Testament is the Greek word *daimonizomai* ("die-mah-nee-zah-mai," Strong's #1139), and it comes from the root *daimon* ("die-moan," Strong's #1142)—which you will recognize as "daemon" or "demon," though the word is often translated "devil" or "devils." It comes from a meaning of "distributing fortunes" (as in divination) and refers to a god or goddess, a lesser deity, or an evil spirit.

Theologians have varying viewpoints on where demons come from. There are three major opinions: 1) that demons are the disembodied spirits of a pre-Adamic race that became corrupted when Satan and his angels fell to the earth; or 2) that they are the fallen angels themselves; or 3) similar to the second theory is that the Nephilim are the offspring of the sons of God mingling with the daughters of men, based on the reading of Genesis 6:1-8 that "sons of God" means angelic beings.

A whole host of material has been presented on these theories, much of which is simply conjecture—though I do not discount the notions entirely—and must be put forth by looking to extrascriptural writings (like the Apocrypha), since the Bible itself does not explicitly state what demons are, other than "evil spirits."

At any rate, for the first and third theories, subsequent to the Flood, these beings perished and lost their physical bodies, but their spirits are still operating from the second heaven (not the realm of God—the third heaven—but a spiritual realm coinciding with the physical realm we live in), and they are now called demons.

What do I think they are, you ask? It doesn't matter to me either way. It might be a mix of all three, for all I know: fallen angels, their offspring, and some kind of disembodied spirit from a race before Adam. Though I do want to say I draw the line with folks claiming they're *human* spirits. When you die, you either go to heaven or hell instantly—there are no ghosts. Any kind of contact initiated from our end with someone who has died is either divination or a manifestation of a demon looking like a person (a familiar spirit.) There is a wealth of verses on what a familiar spirit is—just Google "Bible verses about familiar spirits."

No one can really know for sure if demons are some ancient Sumerian civilization that somehow managed to breach the realm to the second heaven, or whatever is going around these days. It gets a little far-fetched when we start talking about transdimensional travel, and it's a step away from little green men on Mars—or I think they're gray now, whatever. The point is, we have to be *real* careful here that we don't step over into *Star Trek* and boldly go where no man has gone before. If there *are* aliens, they're probably demons; and if they aren't, that's between them and the Lord, so it doesn't concern us in the slightest.

While I don't necessarily have an issue with a pre-Adamic race, or a hybrid race of Nephilim, we cannot be doctrinally dogmatic in either case, because the Bible isn't implicit, though many well-learned theologians cite interpretations of scriptures supporting both schools of thought. I'll leave it up to them to hash it out, and in the meantime, I'll just focus on Jesus' present-day ministry of casting the critters out, no matter what they are.

This isn't a book on demonology, *per se*. But since it *is* a book on deliverance, I want to take a bit here and outline some scriptural points of what I think demons are, or rather, how they operate.

"Possession," to most Christians, is a slippery slope. Rather, I maintain it means to be "under the influence" of the demonic in a particular area of the mind, emotions or body because of an unrenewed, weakened will that gave place to them. To be completely "demonized" suggests to me possession of the most severe order—wherein the demonic has influence in not only the mind, will, emotions and body, but in the spirit as well—which is to be spiritually dead toward Christ; that is, unsaved. I do not believe a born again Christian can be "possessed" of a demon in their spirit, but I do believe one can be influenced by an evil spirit in their soul and body.

If your theology doesn't accommodate that, fine, I'm not here to argue with you. However, after laying hands on thousands and thousands of born again Christians, and seeing them cough and gag when we take authority over a spirit of infirmity or harassment, I cannot be convinced otherwise that Christians—though blood-bought in their spirits—can still struggle with demonic oppression in the other areas of their lives.

My autobiography recounts a graphic deliverance when I was in Bible school from a spirit of rejection—this was *after* I was born again and Spirit-filled. If that bothers you, then let's agree that at the very least, the enemy can badger or harry the redeemed of God in varying levels—otherwise, no Christian would be sick, or depressed, or struggling with a particular sin area, right? We would already be living above the Snake Line, and the present-day deliverance ministry of Jesus Christ would be needless.

Fair enough? All right then, let's discuss what demons are like.

"Then the seventy returned with joy, saying, 'Lord, even the demons are subject to us in Your name.' And He said to them, 'I saw Satan fall like lightning from heaven. Behold, I give you the authority to trample on serpents and scorpions, and over all the power of the enemy, and nothing shall by any means hurt you. Nevertheless do not rejoice in this, that the spirits are subject to you, but rather rejoice because your names are written in heaven.'" (Luke 10:17-20)

The Greek word for trample is *pateo* ("pah-tay-oh," Strong's #3961), which we had mentioned earlier regarding Ephesians 2:10. The root of *pateo* means "to strike or smite with a single blow, to sting," as in to "strike a path." It means to trample down underfoot, to treat with "insult and contempt," "to encounter successfully the greatest perils from the machinations and persecutions with which Satan would fain thwart the preaching of the gospel." Not a bad word, if you ask me.

Serpents are a representation of a spirit that tempts one to sin. We all know snakes attack with their heads, usually baring fangs with a hiss and then lashing out to give unwary travelers a warning strike: "You don't want this!" Very, very rarely does a venomous snake attack without first giving a forewarning in the name of a "dry bite."

Yes, I know there are exceptions and we can only take the analogy so far, but for the purposes of our discourse, we mean the demonic can be snakelike in their activity of enticing us toward sin. My point is the "dry bite," as it were, is to be a warning when we are tempted: "You don't want this!"

First Corinthians 10:13 says, "No temptation has overtaken you except such as is common to man; but God is faithful, who will not allow you to be tempted beyond what you are able, but with the temptation will also make the way of escape, that you may be able to bear it."

This means we don't *have* to step on the snake and get bitten.

The rattle sound should be enough to take our steps elsewhere. Nevertheless, if we do step on a snake's nest (or whatever you call the place they live), Jesus assures us we have been given authority to trample them without being hurt. Concerning our own wellbeing, this authority is provided immediately after sin is cleansed, when we ask for forgiveness and repent (change our mind, our course of action) toward it.

Working in tandem with serpents are scorpions.

"But each one is tempted when he is drawn away by his own desires and enticed. Then, when desire has conceived, it gives birth to sin; and sin, when it is full-grown, brings forth death." (James 1:14-15)

The sting of death comes from giving into sin. When we give place to temptation and fall into sin, we can get stung. Just as in the natural, when stung by a scorpion (I mean the deadly kind), corruption and decay sets in; spiritually speaking, this is guilt and condemnation, two things that keep us below the Snake Line.

Again, thankfully, "If we confess our sins, He is faithful and just to forgive us our sins and to cleanse us from all unrighteousness." (1 John 1:9) That phrase "all unrighteousness" speaks of cleansing us from all the effects or outcome of sin. The power of Jesus' blood, applied in His present-day deliverance ministry, releases us from the consequences of sin—the death and festering putrefaction of a scorpion's sting.

In Luke's Gospel, Chapter 11, when Jesus was casting out a mute demon, some of the people said He was doing so by the power of Beelzebub, the prince of demons (some texts have it

Beelzebul—akin to "lord of the high place," a title for the false god Ba'al, which means "lord", which was then corrupted into Beelzebub as a derogatory slur.) In either case, the etymology of this title for the "ruler of the demons" (Verse 15)—either Satan himself, or one so high up in the demonic hierarchy as to be his second-in-command—is distinctive, but I will spare the space in this book, since it's not really worth giving that much time to.

Suffice it to say, we take the title to mean "the lord of the fly, or the flies," literally in Arabic, "fly master." This is actually a title of mockery and contempt in Judaic tradition, pretty much equating Ba'al to a pile of dung, and therefore, those who worship him are flies who eat excrement. Ergo, the lord of flies.

I think there is a spiritual application regarding demon-worship as a type of "fly." Flies hunt for rotting things, dead flesh, decaying matter to feast upon and in which to lay eggs. Let's face it, maggots are gross. The analogy here is the false doctrines of demons are poisonous seductions, distractions and weights, quite frankly, piles of dung, that hinder the Christian from approaching the Lord's mountain.

The phrases "deceiving spirits" and "doctrines of demons" in 1 Timothy 4:1-2 speak exactly of these types of flies. The word "deceiving" is also translated "seducing" in the KJV, and the Greek word *planos* ("plah-noss," Strong's #4108) means "rover, wanderer," inferring a "tramp or vagabond," one who "misleads another into error, a corrupter or deceiver."

These spirits gently lead one off the path to the Snake Line so that they might waylay the hapless person in a secluded, dimly lit place. It speaks of subtlety, because if a person knew they were being deceived, they wouldn't be deceived. It is corruption through trickery, an act of subterfuge to beguile a person into following their pseudo-truth teachings.

Departing from the faith isn't so much out-and-out rejecting Christ, turning one's back on salvation; but rather, walking out of the narrow line of sound doctrine, giving heed to a whispering, seductive voice that isn't *all* wrong, but just enough to trick someone into following a side trail away from the Snake Line. Over a length of time, the person loses so much of their sense of direction and their idea of boundaries, they are easily ensnared by a highway man laying in wait behind the bushes.

If it was an overt attack, a Christian might be more wary to know they were besieged. But when it is cunningly devious, they can be led astray over time by these doctrines of devils. That phrase "doctrine of devils" (KJV) in the Greek is literally "teachings, instructions, precepts of demons." (See Strong's #1319; #1140.) It is false directions given by an evil spirit, leading one off the right path.

In the Parable of the Sower (Luke 8), Jesus speaks of the "birds of the air" (Verse 5) devouring the seed. We can equate demonic activity as fowls swooping down to gobble up the Word planted within us, so that it doesn't bear fruit. This is akin to the "prince of the power of the air, the spirit who now works in the sons of disobedience..." (Ephesians 2:2) This comes from giving into unbelief and doubt, listening to the lies of the enemy: "'Has God indeed said, "You shall not eat of every tree of the garden"?'" (Genesis 3:1) Being tricked into disobedience is still disobedience.

Remember, the fowls are trying to get us to first *doubt*, then *deny*, and ultimately *disobey* what the Word of God has said. Afterward, what was sown has been gobbled up, and we are left famished.

Further exploring the analogy of fowls, Matthew 24:28 says wherever there's a corpse, that's where vultures gather. The KJV and NKJ render it "eagles," but we know eagles don't normally eat carrion, so the word signifies "vultures," which is the word many translations use. Check out other translations of Micah 1:16 to see the interchangeability of the word.

Vultures feed on flesh, as do demons. The understanding here is that the demonic is trying to invade Christians, looking for manifested flesh (that is, sins of the mind, emotions and body.) Like the reference to James 1:14-15 earlier, conceived lust brings sin. This is a state wherein flesh is not crucified. Flesh cannot be cleansed, nor can it be cast out; it must be subdued, that is, "crucified with Christ." (Galatians 2:20)

Isaiah 59:5 KJV talks about hatching "cockatrice eggs." Now, we know the cockatrice is a mythical beast, supposedly a serpent hatched from a chicken egg, I think, or like a dragon with a rooster's head. But the beast is appropriate to our parallel that demons from without come in to *unite with manifested flesh*. This is a "conception" that later breeds death.

That's why it is so important for us to guard the "ear gate" and the "eye gate" on our walk to the Snake Line. Ear gate means what we hear and listen to. Eye gate means what we look upon. I am speaking of what we habitually, steadily hear and see over a period of time, what we permit to enter into these gates continuously unchecked. Again, we're not talking about a one-time occurrence, but something that we regularly feed our eyes and ears upon.

This is why it is so important to repent (change our mind and stop a particular action) quickly and sincerely. We must close any open doors to the enemy. For what begins as an obsession in the mind can quickly become openly manifested in the flesh, and demons have a legal right to feed on flesh that's "put out there." We must keep our lives hidden in Christ and our flesh crucified and kept under subjection to our spirits.

Song of Solomon 2:15 speaks of "little foxes that spoil the vine." Several Bible commentators remark that these are allegorical of false teachers whispering half truths, and many also hold to the notion that these are "little sins" that end up destroying the roots of the vine. Tying this into the types of demonic activity, we can take this to mean a spirit's activity that attempts to steal what God would have you bring forth.

The adjective "little" in the Hebrew conveys the notion of being young, and therefore "small, insignificant, unimportant." (Strong's #6962) These sins that seem to mean nothing—little white lies, petty theft, wrong motivations and unchecked thought patterns. Things that don't have a "victim," in the sense that we're not being malicious to another, but which still end up damaging the vineyard of your life. *All* sin, no matter how great or "little," must be cleansed by the blood of Jesus.

"Foxes" in the Hebrew means a burrowing animal, perhaps a jackal—something small enough to dig a hole underneath the roots of the vineyard. A lot of interesting commentary has been put down concerning foxes and their love for grapes, so this isn't entirely poetical. But I want to point out the base for the word "foxes" comes from the Hebrew word for the "hollow of the hand" (that is, the palm), which comes from the root to "hollow out." (Strong's #8168) Hence, foxes means burrowers. When the foxes hollow out the roots under the vine, it withers and dies. Like so, the little sins, or being led away from the Truth by the hollow lies of false teaching, kills the plant—your life of abiding in Christ—at the roots. This may be why some of us have such difficulty reaching the Snake Line.

Isaiah 35:7 in the KJV speaks of the "habitation of dragons"—like I mentioned earlier, this that word that is sometimes translated "jackals" as it is in the NKJ. These dragons parched the ground by laying on it, crushing the undergrowth, the grass, reeds and rushes. This speaks of demonic oppression, pressing down, bowing down the "greenery" of our life. By doing so, they make areas of life inoperative, suppressed and held down. Specifically these are *accusations* that the enemy spits out against us—either us accusing ourselves, or others accusing us, or accusing God to us.

Revelation 12 calls Satan the great dragon, "that serpent of old," (Verse 9) and goes on to label him the "accuser of our brethren." (Verse 10)

But notice Verse 11: "And they overcame him by the blood of

the Lamb and by the word of their testimony, and they did not love their lives to the death."

The power over the demonic—and thus the means to proceed on the hidden path to the Snake Line—is firmly rooted in the power of the blood of Jesus being applied to your life, as well as your confession—your evidence given to the Judge of All, who is Jesus Christ. (See Strong's #3056 and #3141, "word of testimony.")

Deliverance is a Process

Recall Joel 2:32 from earlier in the chapter. It is those who call upon the name of the Lord that will be saved and delivered. Yes, God calls the remnant, but the first part of that verse shows us we have something to do in the deliverance process. It doesn't happen "automatically" because we accept Jesus Christ as our personal Lord and Savior—at least not in our soulish area of life.

So what are some keys we can utilize to help us in our great need of seeing deliverance?

Firstly, we need to approach the Lord with humility. We are in no shape to save ourselves, and therefore, it is the height of witlessness to call upon the name of the Lord with an arrogant attitude. I have written pages and pages elsewhere on the importance of humility; feel free to avail yourself of them. While I have not attained, it does not negate the fact that everything we receive from God starts from a broken stance of humbleness.

God knows us better than we know ourselves, so let's cut the charades and be honest with Him and ourselves. We need help, we need deliverance—all of us—in some area of our lives. And we will continue to need it as we walk the Spirit's path. That's why deliverance is a process, a way of life. I'm not saying we need massive deliverance for everything we've ever thought or faced. Not *everything* is a demon, and deliverance is more than that, anyway. Yes, the grace of the Lord is sufficient for us—but we cannot "do away" with the notion of needing our daily bread. It's dishonest before the Lord (and conceited) to think so.

We need to confess our need and confess our sin—great and small—to the Lord. He is faithful and just to forgive us and cleanse us. (Again, 1 John 1:9.) But we need to confess it, we need to ask for forgiveness. It doesn't happen spontaneously and mechanically.

Renunciation is an important part in the deliverance process. We need to renounce—that means to reject, abandon, forsake, refuse, disown, disavow, quit—our own fleshly, or demonically affected, ways and thoughts, our sinful leanings and desires. We cannot cover over our sins.

"He who covers his sins will not prosper, but whoever confesses and forsakes them will have mercy." (Proverbs 28:13)

Lastly, as we wind this chapter down, I want to point out the importance of forgiveness. Harboring unforgiveness is a wide open door for the enemy to come right in and bring all its torment and oppression. Forgive others, and forgive them quickly. You *can* do this, by the grace of the Lord and the help of the Holy Spirit.

"For if you forgive men their trespasses, your heavenly

Father will also forgive you. But if you do not forgive men their trespasses, neither will your Father forgive your trespasses." (Matthew 6:14-15)

Don't hold on to "junk," it's not worth holding on to. Let the Spirit analyze your thoughts and feelings, and when He brings up an element of unforgiveness in your life, let it go. Deliverance is at your doorstep! Work with the process and you'll be well on your way to the Snake Line.

"Now may the God of peace Himself sanctify you completely; and may your whole spirit, soul, and body be preserved blameless at the coming of our Lord Jesus Christ."

—1 Thessalonians 5:23

8

Oppressions of the Enemy

ven though our enemy is defeated, crushed and paralyzed, with only the limited operation we give him through disobedience or ignorance, it doesn't negate the sad fact that the vast majority of us have certain areas of our lives that are harassed by the devil and his brood. In order to progress forward toward the Lord's mountain and the Snake Line, then, we must be made aware of how Satan operates—his tricks and devices that are used to hinder our walk in the Spirit.

Don't let this be a source of condemnation, for that is one of the greatest tactics the devil has in his arsenal against you. Rather, allow the following information to enlighten your spiritual understanding so that you might know what to stand against and exert Christ's already-won victory in that area of your life.

"Then Peter opened his mouth and said: 'In truth I perceive that God shows no partiality. But in every nation whoever fears Him and works righteousness is accepted by Him. The word which God sent to the children of Israel, preaching peace through Jesus Christ—He is Lord of all—that word you know, which was proclaimed throughout all Judea, and began from Galilee after the baptism which John preached: how God anointed Jesus of Nazareth with the Holy Spirit and with power, who went about doing good and healing all who were oppressed by the devil, for God was with Him.'" (Acts 10:34-38)

Three primary ways Satan attempts to assert purloined authority over us is by the roots of spiritual iniquity, physical infirmity and emotional torment—each equating to the three components of your existence: spirit, soul and body.

Nearly all of a Christian's struggle against the enemy takes place in the realm of the mind, will and emotions (the soul) with some "spill over" into the physical realm (sickness and disease.) Most physical illness can be linked to a soulish root—though I want to caution the reader, *not always.* Sometimes a sickness is the attack of the enemy against the body directly, without a soulish cause. But more often than not, there is a link between soulish torment and physical infirmity. So deliverance kind of goes hand in hand with inner healing and divine healing.

The curse of God against the man, woman and serpent of Genesis 3 is generally defined as three roots of iniquity—the wages of sin, which brought death. (Romans 6:23) Collectively, theologians have called these the "bruises of Satan," and they predominately apply to the soulish realm, since this is the gateway the enemy has in which to attack us. These roots are rejection, grief and guilt (or shame.) In other booklets, I have discussed guilt and rejection (see *The Freedom Series: The Wounded Cry* and *Invisible Wounds: Guilt*) and as time allows, I will write a third booklet on grief in the near future. But in the course of this chapter, we'll touch briefly on all three.

Thankfully "the gift of God is eternal life through Jesus Christ our Lord." This eternal life doesn't start when you die—the victories of Christ are to be manifested in your earthly life way before you enter into your eternal life, otherwise there is no point in striving for the Snake Line while we still draw breath on this earth.

"The Spirit of the Lord God is upon Me, because the Lord has anointed Me to preach good tidings to the poor; He has sent Me to heal the brokenhearted, to proclaim liberty to the captives, and the opening of the prison to those who are bound; to proclaim the acceptable year of the Lord, and the day of vengeance of our God; to comfort all who mourn, to console those who mourn in Zion, to give them beauty for ashes, the oil of joy for mourning, the garment of praise for the spirit of heaviness; that they may be called trees of righteousness, the planting of the Lord, that He may be glorified." (Isaiah 61:1-3)

Though prophesied through Isaiah, these are the words of Jesus which He read aloud in the synagogue and proclaimed they were fulfilled on that day. (Luke 4:16-21) His total and complete victory over Satan provides the means with which we may deal with sin, flesh and the demonic—the three great enemies we face in this life.

Sin and iniquity open the door to the demonic by giving it a trespass right to invade. Again, we need to make the distinction between the soul and the spirit. No, I do not believe a Christian can be "possessed" by a demon in their born again spirit. However, the works of the flesh can correlate to a demonic influence inside the soul and body.

Because of sin, the soul and the body are the areas that can become invested in demonic behavior, which has the corresponding "symptoms" of grief, guilt, rejection, bitterness, fear, worry, doubt, condemnation, oppression, harassment, sometimes (not always) mental instability, emotional distresses, and physical affliction through spirits of infirmity.

Again, not *everything* is a demon. It would be much simpler if that were the case, because then we'd simply need to cast it out through the power of the Lord's name, and there would be no more problems. However, I think we, especially in America, don't realize that we confront the demonic more often than we'd like to admit. I believe that if the body of Christ as a whole would deal more swiftly and decisively with the demonic roots behind a lot of our issues, we would be better off. Getting free from the oppressions of the enemy paves the way for the other darkened areas of our lives to become more quickly illuminated by the Spirit, thus hastening our path to the Snake Line.

I do not want to create an element of fear in you, dear reader, that *every* issue you face is a demon. Fear is not godly, because God is love and perfect love casts out fear. (1 John 4:8,18) Rather, I wish to create an element of discernment, which can only come from the help of the Holy Spirit, and an attitude of faith toward God (Hebrews 6:1), which comes by hearing the Word. (Romans 10:17) Discerning of spirits (1 Corinthians 12:10; all kinds of spirits: flesh, demons or *the* Spirit) is one of the greatest gifts we can develop, and sadly one of the most sorely neglected when we take the body of Christ as a whole.

On the opposite side of the spectrum, a spirit of fear—which is a real entity, though not *all* fear comes from a demon; it can be mentally dredged up—robs us by hindering our faith, trying to dominate our outlook on life so that we withdraw from the power of the Lord and turn inward, "hiding out" in the darkness of our own souls instead of under the shadow of the Almighty. Thus, we're easily picked off by the attacks of the enemy.

The torment of fear paralyzes a person into inaction, and thereby inhibits their ability to receive from the Lord, be that in the name of healing, restoration, blessing.

Bruising

Carrying woundings from Satan can hinder our walk with the Lord. If we're limping and favoring a bruise, we move much more slowly. It takes a revelation of the Father's heart toward us to bind up the wounds and heal us so we can move without restriction. The Father's heart is a concept that would require its own book—and indeed, a good portion of *The Dancing Hand of God* is dedicated to this.

But for the purposes of this book, I want to define woundings, or bruises, as the leftover marks of being maltreated by others. They are spirits of abandonment, neglect, rejection, abuse (mental, emotional and physical.) Things that have created a warped perspective of ourselves, or of the Lord to us.

"The spirit of a man will sustain his infirmity; but a wounded spirit who can bear?" (Proverbs 18:14 KJV)

The so-called "death of an expectation" is a wound of grief.

Proverbs 13:12 says, "Hope deferred makes the heart sick, but when the desire comes, it is a tree of life." Many people—Christians are no exception—have suffered the sting of disappointment. I'm talking major crushing of a hope or dream, something that has shaped the course of their very lives. The testings of life can leave people with a bitter taste in their mouths, and they promise themselves never to be "let down" again.

The revelation of the healing anointing—Christ's compassion to see them made well—can bind the wound of grief, but we must make sure we don't become so disheartened that we turn away from the very One who can save us. We need to have a new life restored to our expectations—a hope for the future, an expected end. (Jeremiah 29:11)

The wound of guilt or shame stems from a veiled understanding of Christ's own righteousness within us. Many people labor under a sense of condemnation, as opposed to conviction, for things that they have absolutely no means of ever rectifying to begin with. The past is the past, and it cannot be changed. No matter what rebellious or ignorant thing we may have done in the past, we cannot let it dictate our future. We will never reach the Snake Line always looking over our shoulders.

I don't care what horrible thing you might have done—it seems there is no limit to the depths humanity can sink—all of it must be cleansed by the blood of Jesus Christ, or it can be an open door of the enemy to keep you shackled in the past. Either His blood works for the remission of your sins, or it doesn't. There is no halfway forgiveness.

I'm not saying we shouldn't have a healthy level of regret for our poor or recalcitrant decisions. There is such a thing as godly grief. But to be so bogged down by the past that it mars our future activity is not only ungodly, but thoroughly dangerous, because we cannot be wary of what lies before us, if we're stuck worrying about what has already been left behind.

Of course, you should make restitution when you can; but ultimately, apart from the righteousness of the Lord working in us, we must know that all our own righteousness isn't enough to achieve the Snake Line. Our greatest benevolent deeds executed with the best of intentions aren't enough to save us, so why are we consumed with our shortcomings?

What makes one righteous? Only the Lord Jesus Christ. You're righteous because Jesus lives inside you, and He says you are. It's really as simple as that. We must have a revelation of how God the Father deals with sin that has been cleansed by the blood of Jesus. "As far as the east is from the west, so far has He removed our transgressions from us." (Psalm 103:12) That's *far!*

Righteousness means "right-standing" before the Lord. You either are, or you aren't. Romans 14:17 says the kingdom of God is righteousness, peace and joy in the Holy Spirit. You are either in the kingdom of God or under the domain of darkness, one or the other. (Colossians 1:13)

While you can grow in righteous thoughts and deeds, you cannot come into more right-standing before God than you already are, if you are born again. It's an all or nothing concept. You are either saved, or you aren't.

Now, as this whole book is trying to show, you are *growing* in your understanding of your salvation—certainly in the realm of your soulish life and physical body—but as far as between you and the Father, if you have confessed your sins (whatever they are) and believe in your heart that Jesus' blood is a sufficient enough offering for them, you are square with the Godhead. (Romans 10:9; 1 John 1:9)

I know Isaiah 64:6 says that "all our righteousnesses are as filthy rags," but we also have to keep that in the context of those who "have sinned" and "need to be saved." (Verse 5) It is the iniquities (leanings toward sin) that have taken us away. (Verse 6) All that passage means is, we need a Savior to fix us! We need Christ's blood to blot out our sins. We need Him to uproot the iniquities in our lives. This is the present-day deliverance ministry of Jesus Christ in action! Remember that Verse 4 says God "acts for the one who waits for Him," and He meets the one who "rejoices and does righteousness."

Paul quotes from Psalms and Ecclesiastes when he says, "There is none righteous, no, not one." (Romans 3:10) And he goes on to list *why* no one is righteous. But keep in mind, previously he says, "For what if some did not believe? Will their unbelief make the faithfulness of God without effect? Certainly not! Indeed, let God be true but every man a liar. As it is written: 'That You may be justified in Your words, and may overcome when You are judged.'" (Romans 3:3-4)

He caps that off by saying, "Now we know that whatever the law says, it says to those who are under the law, that every mouth may be stopped, and all the world may become guilty before God. Therefore by the deeds of the law no flesh will be justified in His sight, for by the law is the knowledge of sin." (Romans 3:19-20)

So what's the answer then? God demands righteousness, and if good deeds justify no one, then certainly bad deeds take us just that much further away from righteousness. We're up the proverbial creek, then, right?

Not so. Paul goes on to say:

"But now the righteousness of God apart from the law is revealed, being witnessed by the Law and the Prophets, even the righteousness of God, through faith in Jesus Christ, to all and on all who believe. For there is no difference; for all have sinned and fall short of the glory of God, being justified freely by His grace through the redemption that is in Christ Jesus, whom God set forth as a propitiation by His blood, through faith, to demonstrate His righteousness, because in His forbearance God had passed over the sins that were previously committed, to demonstrate at the present time His righteousness, that He might be just and the justifier of the one who has faith in Jesus." (Romans 3:21-26)

The long and the short of this means we have no basis for guilt and shame if we are in Christ. His victory has made us righteous, and anything that says otherwise is a lie from the enemy trying to plague us with a bruising of grief.

Bruises of rejection usually stem from slandering and cruel sayings, words that have torn us down to build someone else up. Perverse speaking that was intended to cast someone's image to the ground to trample upon it. The tongue is a mighty weapon, for good or ill.

The Power of the Tongue

"The words of a talebearer are as wounds, and they go down into the innermost parts of the belly." (Proverbs 26:22 KJV)

"Wounds" is an interesting word in the Hebrew. Most accurately it means to "burn in" (Strong's #3859)—that is, to scorch someone with our speaking. "Even so the tongue is a little member and boasts great things. See how great a forest a little fire kindles!" (James 3:5)

"Wounds" means to rankle them with what we say. The root of this word means to "gulp down greedily," as in to swallow someone whole by the words coming out of our mouths. This is why the NKJ translates it "tasty trifles." Dainty morsels. To think so poorly of a person's worth that we gluttonously devour them as a tiny snack. This is perverse speaking, and it is a primary weapon the devil uses to hinder God's people.

"And the tongue is a fire, a world of iniquity. The tongue is so set among our members that it defiles the whole body, and sets on fire the course of nature; and it is set on fire by hell. For every kind of beast and bird, of reptile and creature of the sea, is tamed and has been tamed by mankind. But no man can tame the tongue. It is an unruly evil, full of deadly poison. With it we bless our God and Father, and with it we curse men, who have been made in the similitude of God. Out of the same mouth proceed blessing and cursing. My brethren, these things ought not to be so." (James 3:6-10)

We have all been guilty of "cursing men" at some point in our lives, so this applies to anyone reading this book. None of us treat everyone we come in contact with, every time, as someone made in the similitude of God. We do not really understand or appreciate the power that our words have in either helping someone toward the Snake Line, or driving them farther away from it. And the truth is, we'll give an account.

"...For out of the abundance of the heart the mouth speaks. A good man out of the good treasure of his heart brings forth good things, and an evil man out of the evil treasure brings forth evil things. But I say to you that for every idle word men may speak, they will give account of it in the day of judgment. For by your words you will be justified, and by your words you will be condemned." (Matthew 12:34-37)

Oh, how we need deliverance from our tongues! If I could hammer home one valid point in this book on deliverance (and I speak to myself as well), it is we need to be aware of what is said, to us, coming from us, and what we say to God. We are not careful enough in our speech, because it requires great care to keep our tongues bridled. And indeed, it cannot be done without the help of the Holy Spirit. But that doesn't make it of any less importance as we climb the Lord's mountain! The Highway of Holiness is found in how carefully we guard our tongues, or disregard the tongues of others (Satan or the people around us), more than just about any other factor in our walk of life.

"Let no corrupt word proceed out of your mouth, but what is good for necessary edification, that it may impart grace to the hearers." (Ephesians 4:29)

"Death and life are in the power of the tongue, and those who love it will eat its fruit." (Proverbs 18:21)

It's actually quite amazing how much of the Holy Bible is dedicated to admonishing us to watch what we say, and it's one of the easiest things we disregard. Take a moment to study just a few scriptures on the tongue: Psalm 39:1; Proverbs 6:16-19; 12:18; 15:4; 21:23; James 1:26.

According to Matthew 16, the power to bind and loose was given to us—we make this known through the power of our tongue. What we say matters, and how we implement Christ's victory in our lives is directly related to our proclaiming the name of Jesus (and the authority it represents delegated to us) by the power of His blood, and our subsequent position in Him throughout, whereby we claim our right to the *zoe* life of God, which is the principle of the law of the Spirit of life in Christ Jesus. (Romans 8:2) Whew! That's a power packed sentence.

The Fruit of Rebellion

"Now the works of the flesh are evident, which are: adultery, fornication, uncleanness, lewdness, idolatry, sorcery, hatred, contentions, jealousies, outbursts of wrath, selfish ambitions, dissensions, heresies, envy, murders, drunkenness, revelries, and the like; of which I tell you beforehand, just as I also told you in time past, that those who practice such things will not inherit the kingdom of God." (Galatians 5:19-21)

This is pretty much a dirty laundry list of the sad human condition apart from Christ. There is such a wealth of information packed into these verses that I wanted to take a little bit here to define what each of these fruits of rebellion are. Each of these are weapons of the enemy to keep you under the Snake Line. Be wary of these traps, and by the power of the Spirit and the grace of our Lord, keep yourself from them! The present-day deliverance ministry of Jesus Christ is here to eradicate these behaviors out of your thoughts and bodies. Amen!

This list outlines three basic categories of sin: sins of the body, toward yourself; sins of the soul, toward others; and sins of the spirit, toward God.

The first in the list of sins of the body is adultery. This is the Greek word *moicheia* ("moy-hi-uh," Strong's #3430) which is unlawful sexual relations, generally speaking when one or both parties are married to another. This is distinct from fornication, which is *porneia* ("por-nigh-uh," Strong's #4202), and refers to any type of unlawful sexual relations, including adultery, but also homosexuality, incest and bestiality.

Uncleanness is *akatharsia* ("uh-kuh-thar-see-uh," Strong's #167), speaking of the opposite of purity, or the promotion of impure living. This means to be "lustful, luxurious, profligate" or "lewd." To be immoral and licentious.

It is similar to lewdness (lasciviousness in the KJV), which in the Greek is *aselgeia* ("uh-sell-guy-uh," Strong's #766), meaning to promote lewdness. Behavior that incites a bawdy vulgar, coarse response. To be "touchy-feely," lecherous, libidinous. The root of this word apparently refers to an ancient Greco-Roman city, Selge, Pisidia, in modern Turkey whose inhabitants were known for strict morality. Compounding it with the negative "A," it then means *not* Selge, or to live amorally. There might be some basis for the connotation that the word refers to earth's continents, therefore speaking of boundaries. Thus "A" before it means living with "no boundaries." An "anything goes" mentality.

Drunkenness is *methe* ("meth-eh," Strong's #3178), where the word "mead" comes from, implying bouts of drunkenness, being a slave to anything intoxicating.

Revellings in modern vernacular would be "carousing," a revelry. In the Greek, this is *komos* ("koh-moss," Strong's #2970) and can be translated "rioting." It refers to the nighttime wanderings of drunken people cutting loose and playing boisterous music to obscene songs in honor of Bacchus, the god of wine and merriment, or to participating in debauched feasting and drinking parties.

Sins of the soul are sins committed toward others. The first mentioned in Galatians 5 is hatred, which is *echthra* ("eck-thrah," Strong's #2189), meaning "enmity." To find someone bitterly odious, such a strong dislike that one wishes another ill-will; that is, holding a grudge against someone.

Contentions (or variance in the KJV) is *eris* ("eh-riss," Strong's #2054), and it speaks of quarrelsome discord, debating, "strife and wrangling."

Envy (envyings archaically) is the Greek word *phthonos* (something like "faugh-noss," Strong's #5355), which is jealousy at the good fortune of others. It most likely comes from a strengthened root meaning "to pine or waste away," and carries the connotation of being corrupted or defiled, actually "destroyed" by covetousness, resentment and suspicion.

To me, murders (*phonos*, "fah-noss," Strong's #5408), which specifically means to "slay or slaughter," can also convey the act of "killing" the joy of another, spoiling their happiness. Not just taking their physical life, but taking the enjoyment out of their life. Just like adultery, Jesus made it clear that anger without cause, murder in thought, is sin as much as murder in deed. (See Matthew 5.)

Wrath in the KJV is translated "outbursts of wrath" in the NKJ. The Greek word *thymos* ("thoo-mos," Strong's #2372) speaks of "breathing hard with passion" (not in the modern, romantic sense of the word, but feverous, furious rage.) To be filled with boiling, hot anger that soon subsides. Glowing ardor, which Strong's labels, "inflaming wine (which either drives the drinker mad or kills him with its strength.)" That's a potent brew! Interestingly, the root of this word is "to slay," or rather to sacrifice by immolation, just as an animal sacrificed on an altar. Seeing red.

Emulations (jealousies) is *zelos* ("zay-loss," Strong's #2205) and you'll see the word "zeal" or "jealous" in there. To emulate someone is to imitate them, mimic or copy them; to pattern yourself after someone for the purpose of outdoing them, matching them, rivaling them. More than friendly competition, this becomes an obsession to "get one up" on another. Keeping up with the Joneses.

Strife in the KJV is better translated "selfish ambitions" in the NKJ. This word is *eritheia* ("eh-ree-thigh-uh," Strong's #2052) and is elsewhere translated "contention" in the Bible. However, the connotation is "spinning wool," and refers to winning an election by intrigue. It speaks of a contest for superiority, and of provoking or stimulating one (particularly to anger.) Strong's speaks of partisanship (bias, bigotry, prejudice—to be narrow-minded: "my way is the only right way") and fractiousness. Most succinctly, "to put one's self forward," and can imply winning popular opinion by deceit or trickery, the "low arts."

Lastly are the sins of the spirit, which are against God Himself. Of course, *all* sins are against God. David declares, "Against You, You only, have I sinned..." (Psalm 51:4) But specifically, these works of the flesh speak of spiritual dereliction, which God calls harlotry—that is, giving yourself to another spiritually, when He demands you keep yourself for Him only.

This is idolatry, *eidololatria* ("eye-doh-lah-luh-tree-uh", Strong's #1495), stemming from two Greek words meaning "image" and "worship," or properly "serving" as a servant serves the master. This does not just mean bowing down to a carved image. It means to place more admiration and affection on the likeness of a thing, instead of the real thing itself—so speaking of God, it means to serve something other than Him, and that is all-inclusive—*anything* other than Him. Avarice is a type of idol worship, and indeed, any vice that places itself above your love for God.

There can be only One true love of your life if you desire to live above the Snake Line. We, of course, know this conceptually, but in its execution, at one time or another, we—even as Christians—have loved someone or something more than God.

Witchcraft or sorcery is the Greek word *pharmakeia* ("far-muh-kye-uh," Strong's #5331) wherein you'll recognize "pharmacy." In the New Testament, this refers to any type of spell-making, charms, potions, incantations; but it also refers to drugs and poisons. "Getting high" is a form of witchcraft. More than just the blanket term of "magic," it speaks of seduction and deception, leading us back to idolatry.

Seditions or dissensions is *dichostasia* ("day-hoss-tuh-say-uh," Strong's #1370), which is similar to "dichotomy," distinguishing two things that are polar opposites. Light and dark are a dichotomy, good and evil, things that are mutually exclusive. It means stirring up strife and causing division, and the compound word literally means "twice standing": some people standing over here, and some people standing over there, on opposite sides.

It implies creating controversy or an uproar among people. Dividing God's people is a sin against Him because it creates discord, inhibiting His ability to move among them. It hinders what He wants to do, because there are some people who "only believe this way," and others who "only believe that way," instead of people believing in only *one* Way—that is, Jesus. (John 14:6)

Finally, this is how heresies are started. *Hairesis* ("high-rih-sis,"

Strong's #139) is the division that sprouts from a variety of "opinions and aims." It speaks of a party or sect with their own tenets, and literally means "making a choice" or "casting a vote." Of interesting note, the word can mean to take, capture or storm a city.

I do want to point out that when Paul says, "...They which do such things shall not inherit the kingdom of God" (Verse 21), the word "do" is not a single act (see Strong's #4238 and #4160)—it means to "practice" these things habitually and repeatedly. Why I mention this is to clear up any condemnation from a singular act of indiscretion.

This is by no means a license to "do" these things once and get away with it. All sin is sin, one time or a hundred times, and must be confessed, renounced and cleansed. Who knows at what point in time a work of the flesh becomes "repeated and habitual"? Twice? Three times? Ten times? Don't play around here.

But my point is, when we fail, if we immediately bring this to the Lord, deal with it, and endeavor to do it no more—that is much better than "practicing" these things over a period of time, however long that may be.

A lot of people are continually dealing with harassment from the enemy because they are trafficking in these fruits of rebellion—many of them for large portions of their lives.

But what's great about Galatians 5 is that after all the "junk" is listed, Paul goes on to outline the fruit of the Spirit as a dichotomy of the works of the flesh. We know there is just *one* Fruit, that is the Spirit Himself; but as we yield to Him, a harvest is produced which manifests severally as "love, joy, peace, longsuffering, kindness, goodness, faithfulness, gentleness, self-control." (Verses 22-23)

Love, joy and peace are fruit that is harvested for ourselves and could be viewed as good fruit for our soulish lives, to the betterment of our minds, wills and emotions. Longsuffering, kindness and goodness are fruit harvested for others, in our physical, bodily life as we deal with people on a day-to-day basis. Finally, faithfulness, gentleness and self-control is a fruit that is harvested for God Himself, bettering our spiritual relationship with Him. Again, each manifestation of the Spirit's fruit represents a harvest either for the spirit, soul or body, just as works of the flesh reap a harvest in one of those three areas of life.

Thankfully we have a delivering Lord who wants to set us on the narrow, hidden path to His mountain and the shadow of His almighty wings that will cover over us and keep us from working in the flesh, so that a good harvest of fruit is reaped. If we can deal with these issues, and deal with them permanently (as a lifestyle), we can rise to the Snake Line!

"And Jesus came and spoke to them, saying, 'All authority has been given to Me in heaven and on earth. Go therefore and make disciples of all the nations, baptizing them in the name of the Father and of the Son and of the Holy Spirit, teaching them to observe all things that I have commanded you; and lo, I am with you always, even to the end of the age.' Amen."

—Matthew 28:18-20

9

ost sins have a corresponding demon, though not every sin automatically means one has a demon. I believe we've discussed at length in this book that the present-day deliverance ministry of Jesus Christ is also deliverance from the flesh, not just casting out demons. However, it's a fine line here that gets somewhat blurred. The problem is, every manifestation of flesh has the potential of attracting the demonic. And while I don't necessarily think there's a specific demon for every type of sickness or deviant behavior out there, a lot of times there is a link between repeated misconduct or oppression and a "type" of demon.

If you've read *This Present Darkness*, you might be under the persuasion that there is a specific fallen entity roving around out there named "Adultery" or "Pride" or "Murder" for every singular type of sin. More accurately, there are demons of perversion, hatred, etc., that represent a whole host of iniquity.

So while there may not be a demon "named" Diabetes, there are certainly spirits of infirmity that bring about diabetes, or cancer, or arthritis. Demons of addiction, say, may manifest as alcoholism, lust, or rage. There may not be a demon called Schizophrenia, *per se*, but there are definitely demons of mental illness and insanity. There are demons of deception, but maybe not a demon for *every* type of deception out there.

The point is, you don't necessarily need to know the proper "name" of a demon in order to cast it out. How often would an evil spirit answer honestly, anyway? A lot of well-meaning Christians get into trouble conversing with the demonic. And while we see in Mark 5:9 that Jesus *did* ask a demon its name (or perhaps He was asking the man himself), He also told the evil spirits to be silent, because He didn't need any acknowledgement from the satanic kingdom. (Mark 1, Luke 4)

I've seen deliverance sessions take hours because the people administering the deliverance were having a *conversation* with the spirits. "What's your name?" "Bill." "What's your *real* name?" "Susie." "How many of you are there?" "Thirty-seven." "How many *really*?" "Four."

We must recognize our authority in Jesus to command the spirits to leave—that is the point of deliverance, not to get to "know" the demons. Who cares? Get rid of them.

That's not to say an understanding of the root cause behind the vexation isn't important. The discerning of spirits operation tells us what we need to know in order to get to the source of the oppression.

"I cannot stop abusing alcohol no matter how hard I try." Then we're dealing with a demon of addiction. I don't need to know if it's a spirit of vodka or a spirit of whiskey.

As we wind this book down, I just want to reiterate a couple of key points: Psalm 91 teaches us that there is a literal place of existence in our lives that is free from the constant vexations of the enemy. A place where we are so "hidden in Christ" that the devil and his angels are incapable of finding us. We have termed this living above the Snake Line.

This "secret place" is found in an abiding, perpetual resting in the presence of the Lord. I am thoroughly convinced 90% of our issues would be taken care of if we would devote the necessary time of waiting upon the Lord, ministering to Him in praise and worship, serving Him just by remaining under the shadow of His wings.

Now, there is no criticism or chiding in that statement. Very few of us have attained to such a lofty position, but that does not negate the existence of such a position, and I believe we all should be pressing toward that high goal.

One of the primary ways toward that goal is the narrow path on the Highway of Holiness. I think it's fair to say the vast majority of our circumstances are brought about by our own doing. Again, not a critical statement, because *I* fall into that "vast majority" category.

However, I also want to point out again that our enemy is a defeated foe—the power of the cross has crippled the adversary. He is *not* as strong as you think! The Lord has made a public spectacle of him. Don't wait until you see him before God's throne to believe that he has tricked the world into thinking he is stronger than he is!

And never forget we have full and complete access as children of God to come before His throne, ask His forgiveness, repent of our actions, and see His delivering grace manifest in our lives. We can work alongside His Spirit to *enforce* the victory He's already won on our behalves.

The Lord God is longsuffering, patient, kind, full of grace; and while it is just wisdom not to take *any* sin against Him lightly, no matter how small, we also cannot live in a state of fear that any time we make a singular mistake, we are suddenly infested with demons. This book has tried to portray a sound, doctrinal balance—the importance of crucifying the flesh with Christ, maintaining a holy lifestyle, but *not* teaching there is a demon behind every bush waiting to jump on you if you fall short.

More than anything, the present-day deliverance ministry of Jesus Christ is used to teach the child of God discernment. What have our actions permitted? Are we dealing with flesh, or are we dealing with the demonic? Is this a stronghold, or is this a demon who has taken up residence within the stronghold?

All unconfessed sin leaves an open door, and we cannot neglect this. But at the same time, our Father is a loving God and a benevolent King—we *always* have recourse to come to Him in true, heartfelt regret and humility, and He will *always* forgive us! No matter what door we have permitted to be opened, or for how long, the power of Jesus can shut it, if we yield and submit to His dealing and cry out to Him for deliverance.

The present-day deliverance ministry of our Lord is for cleansing our sin, casting out the demonic, and helping us to crucify our flesh in overcoming strongholds. We need His Spirit's guidance to distinguish between the three, and the power of His

Word to separate what is of the spirit, of the soul, and of the body. We have spent a good deal of time in this book outlining the difference between the three facets of our existence, and prayerfully we have shown that in most cases, our issues in life reside in the soulish realm more than any other place.

By outlining the works of the flesh, we have endeavored to show some key areas the enemy tries to feed upon and hinder our walk to the Snake Line. These flesh-works may represent strongholds in our minds, wills and emotions, and it is only the power of the Spirit's operating that can tear them down. We must yield to His pruning for our sakes.

Deliverance is a process, a lifestyle, an attitude of the heart. We need to embrace it and become passionate in its pursuit. We do this by seeking the Lord in an ever-increasing manner throughout the course of our born-again lives.

The most condensed truth I can leave you is: God has given you authority to trample on serpents and scorpions. You have the privilege and right to execute that authority in His name to see deliverance take place in your life. You have the ability to walk in a state of freedom and achieve the high mark of the Snake Line!

Administering Deliverance

Often when I pray with people for deliverance, there is some type of a manifestation. Sometimes people may cough or gag, sometimes they may weep, sometimes they may shout with exuberant joy. All of these are "normal" in the case of deliverance, and we should be open to these types of manifestations, provided the person is set free. In rarer, stronger cases of deliverance, the manifestations may be even "wilder," and I have seen some pretty strange stuff. Normally, this is in the case of strong ties to New Age or occult practices, but I have seen a lot of manifestations across the board.

However, I want to make it clear that there does *not* have to be a manifestation for deliverance to take place, and we should not demand that someone experience one in order for the deliverance to be effective. Like I have taught behind the pulpit, the demonic didn't manifest going *in*, it doesn't necessarily have to manifest going *out*. It just has to leave.

Many times, the people I minister to stand right where they are, call upon the name of the Lord, and believe in faith that the demonic *must* leave as they exercise their authority. Sometimes people feel something break off or lift off, sometimes they do not.

But when I have people call on the Lord for deliverance, a good act of faith is to first command the demonic to leave in Jesus' name, and then I often have them expel with their mouths—breathing out forcefully several times. In Mark 16:17, "cast out" means to expel and carries the connotation of vomiting out something. The root of the word speaks of pouring out fluids or even excreting waste. (Strong's #1544; #906)

Now, I'm not saying you have to upchuck when you go through deliverance, but I think the forceful expelling is a good step of faith for some people.

But I don't believe people need to totally "wig out" during

deliverance, and we should exercise discernment between someone receiving a genuine deliverance that is setting them free, and someone just catering to a demonic manifestation. We shouldn't permit manifestation "just because"—the people need to be set free. Times of deliverance do not need to be chaotic, frenzied or scary—that is not how the Lord operates.

And yet, we see that even in Jesus' earthly ministry, the demonic did manifest. (Mark 1:26; 5:1-20; Luke 4:33; 8:26-39; 9:42) Also note in Acts 8:6-8, the ministry of Philip: "And the multitudes with one accord heeded the things spoken by Philip, hearing and seeing the miracles which he did. For unclean spirits, crying with a loud voice, came out of many who were possessed; and many who were paralyzed and lame were healed. And there was great joy in that city."

There should be a release of great joy and peace, an administration of God's love, when deliverance occurs—it is truly a miracle, one that can often be seen and heard! A sense of deep peace should encompass a person once an evil spirit has left, just an overwhelming *knowing* that they have been set free. Deliverance should *always* be administered from a sense of love, a compassion and desire to see the people set free.

Remember that deliverance is to be a way of life, periodic times of letting the Spirit search your heart to make sure you remain free. It's not so much critically self-examining every time you pray, *looking* for problems, but being open to the examination of the Spirit through the Word from time to time.

All this information can be applied to praying for

self-deliverance or administering deliverance to another person. As a general rule, it is best to have someone stand with you for deliverance, and I admonish you to work within the guidelines of your local church leadership.

If you don't have that operating in your church, look for someone with maturity and wisdom who is able to stand with you for deliverance. Since deliverance is a lifestyle, it is always beneficial to cultivate sincere relationships within your local body of Christ who can pray in agreement with you when needed.

And yet, I recognize that sometimes it's hard to find someone to minister to you at the moment of need. In those instances, remember you have Jesus! And He is all you will need to be set free.

There isn't some set formula for deliverance, a method that works the same way each time, for each person. But there are some general principles to keep in mind.

Deliverance is an extension of the kingdom of God being brought to bear against the enemy. It is because the kingdom is established *now* in our hearts—we carry it with us wherever we go—that we can release the power of that kingdom through the delegated authority of Jesus Christ, who possesses *all* authority in heaven and earth. (Matthew 28:18) The Holy Spirit is the One who is doing the work of deliverance; we are simply executing the authority given to us in the name of Jesus.

Keep your attention on the person, not the demon. Deliverance is an act of love and faith, not "showing off" power. It may work quickly, or it may take some time depending on the spirit and the level of oppression. Demons who have had a trespass right to afflict someone many years are more reticent to leave, but it doesn't matter—they *must* leave. We need to be committed to seeing the deliverance through to the end.

We also need to ascertain the earnestness and sincerity of the person being ministered to. The demon doesn't have to leave, if the person doesn't want it to. God will not *force* deliverance on someone. Maybe the person doesn't want to "keep" their demons, and it could stem from a lack of teaching or understanding; but sometimes, people like their junk, or they're not ready to give it up. We cannot coerce a person into deliverance.

When we are asking for deliverance, the first step is to repent of any unconfessed sins the Holy Spirit brings to our attention. We may need to release and forgive others, we may even need to go to a person we have wronged and make restitution as we are able. This is not a blanket rule, and we must be led by the Spirit. But it is always the smartest thing to go to the Lord to be cleansed of particular sin before seeking deliverance.

Jesus isn't as concerned about the demon as He is about your heart being right before Him. The deliverance part is "easy," but having lordship over your life is what is most important to Him, and that requires humility and brokenness on your part.

When we seek deliverance, we need to be sensitive to the Spirit's prompting. Any open doors need to be renounced and closed—there must be a genuine desire to be free not only from the demonic, but from the strongholds themselves. It leaves the person in a worse condition to cast out the demon, but leave the door—the trespass right for the demon to enter in the first place—wide open.

"When an unclean spirit goes out of a man, he goes through dry places, seeking rest, and finds none. Then he says, 'I will return to my house from which I came.' And when he comes, he finds it empty, swept, and put in order. Then he goes and takes with him seven other spirits more wicked than himself, and they enter and dwell there; and the last state of that man is worse than the first..." (Matthew 12:43-45)

We need to renounce our connection to the "old man," the way of life that opened the door to the vexation—we need to break off the yokes of oppression, and as the Spirit leads, sever any association with generational curses that may have been passed down from our family before us.

A good example of this is, if one's parents were involved in the occult, there can be an iniquity of vexation that is passed down to the children. Or let's say one's parents were alcoholics, there can be an iniquity of addiction in the children that the demonic tries to feed upon. However, not *every* demon is the result of a generational curse, so again, this takes discernment.

Now, a parting thought to get this refocused on the Lord. You need not fear any demon in hell. Don't go picking fights where you don't need to, but when you are confronted with a true need of deliverance in your life, or in the life of someone the Lord directs you to, you need to remember that there is One who has gone before you. One who has defeated and rendered inoperative all of the forces aligned against your soul, your joy, and your life.

There is a King above all kings who has overcome the world and who has given you the distinct privilege of calling upon His name and all that it represents—the entire kingdom of heaven in all its power and might—to come to bear on your behalf. His Word and His Spirit are waiting to set you free. Everything you will ever need can be found in Him, and He is desiring to show you His present-day deliverance ministry.

Call upon Him and learn to live above the Snake Line!

Printed in the United States
By Bookmasters